Sink Reflections

By Marla Cilley — The FlyLady

BANTAM BOOKS

New York   Toronto   London   Sydney   Auckland

SINK REFLECTIONS
A Bantam Book

PUBLISHING HISTORY
Bantam trade paperback edition / October 2002
Bantam trade paperback reissue / March 2004

Published by
Bantam Dell
A Division of Random House, Inc.
New York, New York

ISBN 0-553-38217-9

Manufactured in the United States of America
Published simultaneously in Canada

BVG   14   13 12   11   10 9   8 7

Dear FlyLady,

Wanted to let you know about the wonderful B&B my husband and I stayed at this Memorial Day weekend. The small but simply furnished kitchen was well stocked with delicious healthy snacks and meals. Homemade waffles and blackberries were served from a beautiful clean kitchen. The living areas and bedrooms were furnished with fresh plumped pillows, lovely matching sheets and down comforter, and scented candles everywhere.

The bathroom—ah. . .bubble bath, lotions, and fresh white towels. The library was stocked with books, magazines, and yoga videos. Best of all, my husband and I spent time together with no interruptions, chores, or traffic.

Okay—you guessed it. . .Thanks to you—this is my home. Thank you! Thank you!
Laura from California

This book is dedicated to:

YOU,

who have suffered in silence, thinking

that you were the only one in the world

who lived in CHAOS!

Contents

FlyLady's Buzzzzz Words

Just before you begin this book, I want you to know a few terms we use in our community. Some have been coined by us for the FlyLady program and others have come from our wonderful members. All of them will be used throughout the book and as you learn to declutter your home and life, they will become an important way we communicate with each other. You can call them buzz words or jargon or whatever you want.

So here goes:

BABYSTEPS: Always remember: BabySteps! I do not want you to be burned out by doing too much too fast. This is a big problem for all of us. We want it done now. I am here to tell you that this process is going to take time. We will eventually have a clean and organized home, but first we have to learn some routines. Do a little every day.

"BEFORE BED" ROUTINE: This is one of our most powerful tools. This is the most important routine of the whole day! It is not the only one, but it starts you in the right direction every morning. There are also Morning Routines. You will see how this is done in Chapter Five.

CHAOS: Can't Have Anyone Over Syndrome. This is just what it sounds like and you'll learn how to finally conquer this widely shared fear in Chapter Two.

CONTROL JOURNAL: This is a special, customized system to help you stay on track with your daily activities. You build it yourself. It is so important there is an entire chapter (Six) devoted to it. It is just a 3-ring binder to hold your routines in one place.

FIVE-MINUTE ROOM RESCUE: This is one of the tools that FlyLady suggests that you use to clear a path in your worst room. You can identify this room easily by thinking, "which room would cause me to turn bright red if anyone saw it?" Work on this room for 5 minutes for 27 days and it will be the first stop on your home tour!

FLY & FLYING: One of our dear members coined it for me: FLY means Finally Loving Yourself!

FLYBABIES: New members are called "FlyBabies." Keep in mind, you are not behind as a FlyBaby, you are just getting started. I don't want you to think you have to catch up with anyone. You jump in where you are.

FRANNY: A symbol of the sad person within us all when we are surrounded by clutter and CHAOS.

GOD BREEZE: On our first date my husband, Robert, told me about God Breezes. Imagine yourself in a little sailboat on a calm lake. Now think about the vision of God as being the Ole North Wind. If you have your sails up when the breeze comes, you can go where it takes you. If you don't, you are dead in the water.

HOME BLESSING: Each week we spend about an hour "blessing" instead of "cleaning" our home by setting a timer for ten minutes for each of 7 jobs: Change sheets, Vacuum, Dust, Cull magazines, Mop, Empty all the trash, Polish mirrors and doors.

HOT SPOT: Any area, but usually one that is clean. Yet, as soon as you lay one piece of paper on it, the paper will begin to multiply and before you know it, the surface will be covered. I have several: my dining room table, the end of a kitchen counter, the coffee table, an end table, a chair in my bedroom, and my cedar chest. Do I need to say more? You have them too.

MORNING ROUTINE: This is the few items you write down to establish as a habit when you first get up in the morning.

SHE™ (Sidetracked Home Executives): This is a concept from a book written by Pam Young and Peggy Jones (*Sidetracked Home Executives: From Pigpen to Paradise*). In fact they came up with some of the underlying principles of the FlyLady system and have endorsed the way I teach it. Pam & Peggy have changed my life through their books, humor, and wonderful attitude toward living. They first developed the idea of "Zones." A very in-depth explanation of Zones and how to use them is the subject of Chapter Nine. You can access their site from FlyLady.net.

STUFF: This is a shorthand buzzword we use for Something That Undermines Family Fun.

27 FLING BOOGIE: A tool to declutter your house 27 items at a time.

Other Peculiar Terms

BO:	Born-Organized Person
DD:	Dear Daughter
DH:	Dear Husband
DS:	Dear Son
LOL:	Laughing Out Loud
Payroll SHE:	A person who works outside the home
SAHM:	Stay At Home Mom

Acknowledgments

We are each put into a tiny boat when we are born and set on our journey through life. I was introduced to God Breezes on my first date with my husband, Robert, in 1996. As we enjoyed our five-hour dinner on his side porch, Robert described being in this boat, sitting in a large body of water. He explained that we all have choices in our lives, saying: Imagine God as the picture of the Ole North Wind with his cheeks puffed out to blow His mighty breath your way. Now think of yourself as being in that little boat with a sail. It is your choice to raise your sails and let God's Breeze power your journey in the direction of your choice or let the wind pass you by.

We are all little sailboats. Robert and I had been directed toward one another all of our lives. That day, we met in the vast sea and have continued on our journey together. He is my life partner and soul mate. With our eternal love, we opened our sails full out in order to take advantage of the slightest breeze.

Special people love us on our way. My Grandmother has always been the mast of my little boat. She has taught me the importance of doing what is right. As she always says, "Pretty is as pretty does," and "If you do what is right, God will take care of you!" Granny, I have clung to your words and they help hold my sail for God's Breezes. Thank you for teaching me to shine my sink.

My sisters, Paddi and Deena, have always been part of my crew. They cheer me onward and allow me to just be their sister. Thank you both for helping to keep me afloat. My son, Justin, and his lovely wife, Emily, are encouraging us too. He has always been a born-organized child and could not really understand what Mom's problem was. As I have cleared out clutter and found peace, he has been shocked at the difference in our home. I love his surprised look each time he enters our calm home. He was the reason I found Pam and Peggy and the *Sidetracked Home Executives* when he was small. I wanted him to have a home that was orderly and a mom that was not a nervous wreck. Thank you, Pam and Peggy, for the tools to give my son this gift as a child and for your ability to help so many people with your words. You have blessed us all. Without you, none of this would have been possible.

Early on our FlyLady Cruise, I received a God Breeze message from someone that offered to help me. At the time Robert and I were cruising along at a fair clip, but I knew we would need some help soon. Kelly volunteered for the job. So I began to test the waters to see if she knew what our mission was. Every question was answered as if I had written it myself. Robert actually thought I was responding to them. She passed the test with FLYing colors and has become my trusted first mate. Thank you for being my best friend, Kelly, and helping us on our journey. Tom is Kelly's husband, and he cuts right to the heart of most matters with his wry wit and conservative personality. I am grateful for his input and his support of Kelly.

Right when we thought we were struggling and couldn't seem to find a breeze anywhere, along came Cindy. Kelly and I received Cindy's offer to help write our book in an e-mail, and I picked up the phone and called her. I knew after our first conversation that God had sent her to assist us. We were overwhelmed with the development of the website and even though we could not pay her, she was willing to sign on for our cruise. She is our navigator and cruise director. She can handle the details that escape me. Thank you, Cindy, for listening to your God Breezes. Between you, your wonderful husband Barry, and your porch night dates, you have given us many great ideas. We are in for a fun ride together. You help keep the joy in sailing.

As we travel, other sailing vessels have joined us. Dana crossed our path on her way to help flood victims. Her kind heart touched our lives and now she is sailing alongside of us. Thank you, Dana, for helping us with the thousands of messages we receive. Your words comfort many people who are trying to find their way out of CHAOS. Sometimes all anyone needs is to know someone cares. You listen!

Michael blew into our lives to design our new ship. He is responsible for the inner workings of FlyLady.net. Thank you, Michael, for helping us to touch so many lives. You keep us gliding smoothly through the water. You comfort us when the seas get rough and prepare the way for many more passengers. Just knowing that you are as close as a computer gives me peace. You have built a sturdy ship!

We had been FLYing by the seat of our pants for several months when Cindy had the God Breeze to contact the publisher of the best calendar for families. Thank you, Joanne, for giving us an opportunity to share your More Time Mom's Calendar with our members. They love it as we do. May our journeys coincide for many years to help people find the peace they deserve.

We have had many God Breezes on our journey, but there have been times when the Breeze has been a God Hurricane. Three months after we self-published our first version of *Sink Reflections*, the God Breezes filled New York. Michelle Tessler of Carlisle & Company got our book into the hands of Danielle Perez at the Bantam Dell Publishing Group. Robert and I were honored to have Irwyn Applebaum and Danielle enjoy a sunset on our back deck: No words needed. Thank you, Irwyn, for your No Whining rule. You are going to help us relieve the CHAOS all over the world.

As we have made our journey, many members have touched us. One member who has given me more than I will ever give to her is Victoria. Thank you, Victoria, for your purple puddles (tears) and hugs over these many months. You keep me focused on why we are on this journey.

Introduction

Dear Friends:

Welcome to the world of FlyLady! I am Marla Cilley, also known as the "FlyLady," and I am here to help you. I am here to tell you how to help reduce and remove the CHAOS and disorganization in your homes and lives. How do I know how bad it really can be? I have been there, and in this book you will hear my story and the journey that I have taken. I have found a way to replace chaos and disorganization with peace and joy.

A few years ago I hit bottom and, friends, let me tell you there is no place lower than where I was. I realized that one day my home was full of clutter, my sink was overrun with dirty dishes and I looked like a truck had just run over me. I know the sheer embarrassment of having an unexpected visitor show up at the door. I have pretended that I was not home or only talked to the visitor on the porch because there was no way that I could let them in my home.

How do you know if you need this book? Ask yourself if any of these descriptions could apply to you:

1. You live in what we call CHAOS (Can't Have Anyone Over Syndrome).

2. Your husband is getting ready to walk out the door, because he can't live like this anymore. (Or even worse, Social Services is knocking at your door.)

3. Your in-laws are coming for a visit and you are desperate.

4. You are always in a bad mood and you don't know why.

5. You yell at your babies.

6. You can't find anything in the house.

7. The housekeeping service is costing too much but you don't know what you would do without them.

8. You got up in the middle of the night, tripped over something, and found yourself on the floor.

9. You caught the baby eating something that had been on the floor for a couple of days.

10. Your windows are so dirty that you can't tell if it is cloudy or sunny outside.

11. The holidays were a chaotic mess and you are determined not to go through that again.

If you answer yes to even only one of the above, you can benefit from this book. Besides making these things (and much more) disappear from your life, this book will help you FLY— Finally Loving Yourself.

I got my act together one BabyStep at a time and this book will help you do the same. Through the help of Pam Young and Peggy Jones, the authors of the book *Sidetracked Home Executives,* I was able to get up out of my own chaos and begin to help others do the same. As I began our e-mail mentoring group, more and more people came for help and the group evolved into the FLYLady system. We now have a website for our members (www. FlyLady.net) to help them and to continue to teach them to find peace.

This book is for anyone who has a home and is looking for help managing the clutter and chaos. Your home did not become a mess overnight and it will not get clean in a day. But through a series of lessons and tools that I can give you, you will see a light at the end of the tunnel. This book will show you how to take small BabySteps to create routines, how to declutter, how to take large overwhelming chores and break them into manageable missions and, the most important of all, how to bless your home and family.

FlyLady is now a team effort that has several "FlyLadies" to help with our community. You will read more about them throughout the book. This book is my labor of love for anyone that has found themselves overworked, over extended and living in CHAOS. With the use of this simple little book, you will be able to change your own life and find the peace you have been searching for. I do not have a magic wand that I am going to wave over you and make your life different. This is all a process of establishing new and effective habits that will transform your home from the turmoil you have been struggling with to a home of tranquility which will then allow you to transform your life. When I started mentoring my only goal was to help just one person.

Are YOU ready to FLY?

Marla Cilley — The FlyLady
March 2002

FlyLady's 11 *Commandments*

1. Keep your sink clean and shiny.

2. Get dressed every morning, even if you don't feel like it. Don't forget your lace-up shoes.

3. Do your Morning Routine every morning, right when you get up. Do your Before Bed Routine every night.

4. Don't allow yourself to be sidetracked by the computer.

5. Pick up after yourself. If you get it out, put it away when you finish.

6. Don't try to do two projects at once. ONE JOB AT A TIME.

7. Don't pull out more than you can put back in one hour.

8. Do something for yourself every day, maybe every morning and night.

9. Work as fast as you can to get a job done. This will give you more time to play later.

10. Smile even when you don't feel like it. It is contagious. Make up your mind to be happy and you will be.

11. Don't forget to laugh every day. Pamper yourself. You deserve it.

Sink Reflections

Your First BabyStep— Where to Begin

I was tempted to start by explaining why this book is different from all the other cleaning and organizing books that are now cluttering your bookshelves, being used to level the dining room table, or holding down a pile of clutter! But I won't; the FlyLady program is not about cleaning. It is about changing your life to make it more rewarding and leading to a more important goal, to FLY, or Finally Loving Yourself. This is a concept we will talk about throughout this book.

I started helping others through mentoring on the Internet and that help evolved into the FlyLady system. I am an avid fly fisherman and instructor. When I first started going online I needed a name, so I chose FlyLady. Since then FlyLady has taken on so many different forms. People ask me, "Are you THE FlyLady?" Friends ask each other, "Do you do FlyLady?" and on the Internet there are groups of FlyBabies that gather and chat with each other.

This book begins where anyone who becomes a member of FlyLady starts: with a BabyStep. We call this becoming a FlyBaby. And as you use this book, each of your BabySteps will add up. You will lose the feelings of guilt and failure that you've been nurturing. Your clutter will vanish and your life will change forever.

"Your home did not get dirty overnight and it is not going to get clean in a day."

I can hear you now, "What do I do first? Where do I start? My home is a total disaster and there is no way it is ever going to get clean!" Before you start, pencil in today's date on the inside of the back cover. This is the day you are beginning to FLY. You will know why soon enough. I know you are ready to get started, but hold your horses, because I don't want you to crash and burn. We ARE going to begin with a cleaning task. You just have to have faith that this is the best way to start. **Your home did not get dirty in a day and it is not going to get clean overnight.**

With that warning to be kind to yourself, here is your very first assignment. **It all starts with a shiny sink.**

First BabyStep: shine your sink

I know that you don't understand why I want you to empty your sink of dirty dishes and clean and shine it when there is so much more to do. It is so simple. I want you to have a sense of accomplishment. You have struggled for years with a cluttered home and you are so beaten down. I just want to put a smile on your face. When you get up the next morning, your sink will greet you and a smile will come across your lovely face. I can't be there to give you a big hug, but I know how good it feels to see yourself reflected in your kitchen sink. So each morning this is my gift to you. Even though I can't be there to pat you on the back, I want you to know that I am very proud of you.

This is how to shine your sink; we like to call it Shiny Sink 101: *(Note: If you have a special colored or decorative sink, check on your warranty for specific cleaning instructions.)* With ceramic sinks you may not be able to see your reflection, but your heart will be shining because it's clean! You will still smile!

Do not complain or whine that you can't do this because it is full of dirty dishes and nasty water. I am not telling you to wash the dishes; all I want is for you to set the dirty dishes on the counter so you can get to the bottom of your sink. With an empty kitchen sink before you, I know you don't know what to do or where to start so I am going to give you specific instructions on this. You should also know that I have heard every excuse in the world when it comes to sinks, and I know that you may be a bit doubtful about this. Just trust. Even old sinks can look new again with a little elbow grease. BE SURE AND RINSE WELL BETWEEN EACH STEP since mixing chlorine-based products with household ammonia-based products can be toxic!

1. Take all the dishes out of your sink.
2. Then run some very hot water in the sink, to the rim. Pour a cup of household bleach (e.g. Clorox) in the hot water. Let it sit for 1 hour. Wear gloves and don't get it on your clothes.
3. Rinse your sink well.
4. Get some cleanser: Comet, Ajax, or Baking Soda and scrub your sink. Do not use ammonia-based products such as Windex with these.

5. Take a sharp edge and clean around the rim of the sink, just like you would clean dirt out from under your fingernails.

6. Clean around the faucets too. You may need an old toothbrush or dental floss.

7. Now get out your window cleaner (I use Windex) and give it a good shine.

8. If you still don't like the way it looks, then you could try some car wax. Just know in your heart that you have cleaned it very well and know it doesn't have to be perfect. Our perfectionism is what got us in this situation.

9. Every time you run water in your sink take your clean dishtowel and dry it. I lay out a clean one every night with my bedtime routine. Before you know it you will be doing this every time you leave your kitchen. The rest of the family will too. No more water spots. You will have a clean and shiny sink.

10. Don't be upset if someone doesn't take as much pride in your sink as you do. You have done the hard part. You will never have to go through this process again. Daily maintenance will keep it looking this way. Just be sure and tell your family what you are doing, otherwise they will think you have gone crazy. Your family cannot read your mind!

11. If you don't have a dishwasher, don't worry. A dishwasher is just a dirty dish disposal. Clean out a place under your sink and put a dishpan in there. Teach your family that instead of putting their dirty dishes and glasses in the sink, to place them in the dishpan. Get into the habit of putting your dishes away as soon as they have been washed and dried. No more leaving the dish drying rack on the counter or in the sink. Put it away under the sink when you have finished. If your old ones are nasty, you may want to soak them in the sink full of bleach water at the same time you

soak the sink, or go buy yourself a new set. You deserve it as a reward for shining your sink. You are worth a couple of bucks.

12. To ensure that your family remembers this, put a note in the sink. It will get their attention and remind them where to put the dishes. Be patient! They have never been taught either. It is going to take some practice.

"Keep your kitchen sink empty and shining. This works. I don't know why, but a beautiful sink to greet you each morning starts your day with a smile."

Now, if you have a stainless steel sink, I recommend all of the above directions with one added. After you soak it, rinse well and use a steel wool pad to scrub it. This will buff the finish. It will look like new. If you still can't get it to shine after the Windex, then put a light coat of wax, lemon oil, or olive oil on it. I mean just a tiny bit on a cloth and rub it. This will make you smile. Some people have had very good results from cleaning solutions used to keep bar tops clean.

This is your very first BabyStep—to keep your sink clean and shiny on a continual basis.

Aren't you impressed with yourself? Wasn't that easy?

So, what is next? I know you are chomping at the bit to get more than just your sink clean; HOLD YOUR HORSES!

You have another important homework assignment that is going to become a way of life.

You will rediscover the joy of wearing shoes. And it will make every BabyStep just a bit easier. Several years ago I worked for a direct sales cosmetics company. One main rule for that company was that you could not make a single phone call in the morning unless you were totally dressed, and I mean really dressed! All the way to dress shoes. The reason behind this duty was that **you act different when you have clothes and shoes on.** You are more professional. The customer can tell when you don't feel good about the way you look. Even when you think you do.

So if getting dressed makes that big of an impression on someone that can't even see you, then what is going to happen to those that can see you, mainly yourself? Putting shoes that lace up on your feet are better than slip-ons or sandals because they are harder to take off. Instead of kicking your shoes off for a quick snooze on the couch, you actually have to go to a bit more trouble. Maybe in that short instant you will realize that there is something more that you can do. With shoes on those feet of yours, your mind says, "OK, it's time to go to work." You have no excuse for not taking the trash out or putting that box of giveaway stuff into the car. You are literally ready for anything.

"We do what we can today and then we do a little more tomorrow. BabySteps."

Believe me, when you get that call from school that your child needs you, or that dear friend calls up and says that she needs to talk, "Can we have lunch?"— you are ready! Including shoes.

I see this problem more in the SAHMs (Stay At Home Moms) because often they don't have to leave the house and it is not necessary to get dressed every morning. Only their children are going to see them. I want you to listen very closely. You have the most important job of all, raising productive adults. NOW, do you want your children to remember that Mom didn't get dressed until it was time for Dad to get home? Or do you want your children to have to answer the door because you are still in your pajamas and bathrobe? If you would look at your day just like a person working outside the home and realize that the jobs around the house will take as long as you let them (all day in most cases because you allow it), you would get off your "Franny" and get dressed all the way to shoes. Because it is time to go to work.

There is one other great benefit to wearing shoes. Two summers ago was the first time I successfully did this for more than a week or two. It was the first summer time I didn't have cracked and bleeding heels. **Many rewards are waiting. Now put those shoes on.** I don't want to hear, "Well, I don't wear shoes in my house." Well, you do now, sister! Buy or clean up a pair just for that reason. These are your FLY shoes, your home blessing shoes. Step out in faith with me on this issue and I promise that you will see a difference.

The Next BabyStep: choose your clothes for tomorrow

Before you go to bed, I want you to think about what you are going to be wearing tomorrow. What is the weather report and what does your schedule include?

This is such a simple task but it can save you precious minutes when you are rushing around in the morning. So take a few moments and pick out something that you like to wear. From this moment on, sweats and frumpy clothes are not to be worn for daily attire. I want you to feel like a million dollars and that doesn't happen in clothes that don't fit and are not flattering. This is not an excuse to go out and buy a new wardrobe, but you could

7

pick up a couple of items that you love to add to your closet.

Wasn't that easy?

Now your sink is shining, your shoes are on your feet, and your clothes are picked out for tomorrow. (If you have not done this yet, then what are you waiting for? Your transformation is not going to happen by osmosis.)

With snugly laced-up shoes, let's continue. You bought this book looking for a change in your home; this is not going to happen unless you make the effort. Oh, and by the way, if you are reading this and it is past 11:00 PM then put the book down after you read the next paragraph. I want you to go to bed at a decent hour. Your rest is as important as anyone else's in the house. You know how cranky children get when they haven't had their naps. You are not different.

Your next assignment is for tomorrow morning.

When you get up, your first priority is to get dressed to shoes, fix your hair and face. I don't want you to stay in your pajamas all day. Getting dressed will help you feel better about yourself. You have to be dressed to FLY!

I told you it was easy. But let's explore this a bit more.

What are the final touches that make you feel special when you are getting dressed? It could be cleaning and moisturizing your face, putting on makeup if you wear it, fixing your hair, donning a pair of earrings, or placing that string of pearls around your neck. It could also be a spritz of your favorite fragrance, the perfect color of lipstick, or using a sweet smelling bar of soap in your bath.

One other more intriguing possibility could be the undies that you put on that give you that special feeling all day long. Right? After my mother's death at Christmas 2000, one member told me about her prim and proper Southern Mom who would not leave the house without her red lace panties. Our web editor/jack-of-all trades, Cindy, is an engineer and underneath her steel-toed boots, jeans, sweatshirt, hardhat and jumpsuit, she wears her lace teddy. Isn't that just the perfect start to a day?

Decide what you can do to make you feel special each morning.

Each and every one of you is special to me! My goal is that you will feel this worth for yourself. If your outsides look good, your insides feel good. If your insides feel good, you can do anything! The sky is the limit! I want you to shine too!

Now we're ready for another BabyStep.

First take a Preflight Check:

✓ Have you shined your kitchen sink?

✓ Are you dressed with laced up shoes?

✓ Have you fixed your hair and face?

✓ Have you picked out your clothes for tomorrow?

✓ Did you go to bed at a decent hour and get plenty of rest?

"You are never behind. Jump in where you are!"

Dear FlyLady...

Today I am wearing shoes and socks because you say: JUST TRY IT. It's so weird; my ATTITUDE is different this morning :-) I hate how stubborn I can be when it comes to changing, but I am changing, one pair of shoes at a time...
:) a happy FlyBaby from Alaska

Dear Flylady,
Well, I am well into my second week of shoe-wearing! It really has been nice. On Sunday I took the day off from shoe wearing. My feet and my legs were aching! "Where are my shoes?? I need them! Please put them back on!" Funny, huh? I didn't realize how nice it was on my feet and legs to have on shoes until I wore them for a week straight and then did not wear them! WOW!!! Simply amazing! Sometimes during the day my feet will cry out "Where are my shoes?" I will look down to discover my bare feet. Usually I find my shoes under the table or under my desk. Funny! Like I told you in my "whine session," I saw no point in wearing shoes. I am a barefoot girl and I work without shoes. Now I see a point and great benefit and I thank you for your encouragement! I am still a barefoot girl, I just keep my bare feet in shoes! :-) I had my toes done and bought some fun sandals for the pool! What a reward!!! Thank you again!
A happy barefoot girl in shoes,
Kipplyn from Oklahoma

Ah Ha! That's all I can say! I joined the FlyLady list about 2 weeks ago, but haven't done anything more than read the e-mails ... I kept reading all the posts about wearing shoes, and I thought, "what a hokey thing to do, wear shoes?" ... like, How was that going to help me?? But the continued posting about it made me think, "Hmm, maybe there's SOMETHING to the whole shoe thing." So today, finally, I'm wearing my shoes. How amazing! The effect was immediate. I feel taller, so therefore less dumpy, and therefore, more capable!! Also, wearing shoes is like tying a string around a finger — the mere presence of them reminds me to get off my Franny and do something! I still haven't got my sink shiny, but I'm getting there (I have a toddler and a baby, so all the desire in the world sometimes won't overcome their schedule, and my need to feed, change, clothe, etc.). I know where my laundry is, and I've cleaned the bathroom. It's still morning, so that's not bad.
Glenys from Alaska

First of all, thank you, thank you, thank you!!! I feel like a new person! My house looks MUCH better already, but more importantly I feel HAPPY! Who knew that a pair of Keds, some lipstick, and a shiny sink could have such an impact on my soul!
Thanks & God Bless,
Pamela from New Jersey

2 Let's Talk About CHAOS and Clutter

What does the word CHAOS mean to you?

Consider these questions:

Do you literally live a life where a cluttered home has given you something we call **Can't Have Anyone Over Syndrome** or **CHAOS**?

If clutter has made you a prisoner of your home, think about this:

- Does clutter affect you mentally?
- Does clutter affect you physically?
- Does clutter affect your social life?

Is your perfectionism one of the main reasons for clutter and chaos in your life and home?

I suspect that the answer to all of the above is a resounding yes! You are not alone, virtually all of the members of our community have been where you are now. They have taken their BabySteps and clutter and chaos are on their way out, and order and happiness are taking their place. What is it that keeps you from conquering the clutter and CHAOS? You get so caught up in all the reasons why you can't take care of it that you just give up and settle for living this way. Perfectionism will keep you from ever getting out of the CHAOS. This process of BabySteps is all about progress not perfection. You will read about perfection throughout this book. No one is perfect and it is an unattainable goal to set for yourself. Often while answering e-mails from our members I respond with a message that bears repeating for this book:

Dear Friends:

I have found over the last 2 years that PERFECTIONISM is the main reason our homes are in bad shape or CHAOS! PERFECTIONISM is the reason we are depressed and PERFECTIONISM keeps us from making things better.

Robert had a wonderful geometry teacher in high school. She taught him, "Anything worth doing is worth doing WRONG!" This is where I got my saying, "Housework done incorrectly still blesses your family."

As Robert walked out the door for work this morning, he said, "I just had a thought and it sent chills down my spine." I said, "WRITE!" This is what he wrote:

Do you hear your Mother's or Whoever's voice saying, "That's not good enough, you can do better than that. Go back and do it right!" It really didn't matter how nice a spin they put on it. The message came through loud and clear: "Anything less than perfect is unacceptable!" And the horrible extension: "Unless you are perfect, you are not good enough." Or "Not Worthy of Being Loved!!!"

Is this what you have suffered with your whole life?

Well, I have news for those voices in your head. We all fall short of the glory, as the Bible says. Let he who is without sin cast the first stone. We are IMPERFECT BEINGS AND PRAISE GOD FOR OUR IMPERFECTION. He made us and He loves us regardless.

Now, when are you going to Finally Love Yourself enough to say, "I cannot live with this perfectionism any longer. I have got to stop..."?

Are you ready to FLY, Finally Loving Yourself? Let go of your Perfectionism and start to live without fear of being rejected.

—FlyLady

P.S. When I used to be a stained glass artist, I would find myself paralyzed in perfection. So much so that I would make myself sick. It would take hundreds of hours to finish one piece. Finally I realized that I needed to make a few mistakes. Just do some things that the unskilled eye would never notice. This helped me to let go of my perfectionism and sell my work. I always had my own signature mistake in the bottom right hand side. A piece of glass turned with the wrong side out.

I can hear the sighs already!

I know you don't believe that your home can come together. So I am going to ask you some questions that will allow you to examine the stress with which you are living so we can see just how clutter invades every part of your life:

- Do you find yourself standing in the middle of your kitchen turning in circles, not knowing what to do first and trying to do several things at once?
- Are you constantly losing things: your keys or your purse?

- Does your tone of voice shock even you when you are speaking to your children or your spouse?
- Do you have frequent bouts of illness as well as an overwhelmingly helpless, tired feeling?
- Have you always struggled with organization and think that you are hopeless because you weren't "born organized"?
- Do you think you are the only person in a world of born organized men and women that can't keep a nice home?

I am here to tell you: you are not alone and there is help for your perfectionism. What!? You are not a perfectionist! As strange as it may seem, I will guarantee that you have traits that those so-called perfectionist, Born-Organized People (BO) have. There is a fine line that separates you from BOs and it has to do with where we measure up on the perfectionism tally.

"You can't organize clutter!"

BOs tend to be compulsive about getting it clean and keeping it that way, while some of us won't even start a job unless we have enough time to do the job correctly. So we do nothing! Or we are trying to do too many things at once and nothing ever gets finished so we just give up and say, "What's the use?" We want the same things that BOs want, but we don't know how to get from this messy home to the huggable home that we desire.

I'll bet you can identify with this too: when you were a child, you were told to go clean your bedroom. You would stand in the doorway with a puzzled look and your mother would fuss because you were doing nothing. Poor baby, you didn't know where to start and your mother had no clue what your problem was. So you have been told many times that you were lazy! This is the last time you will ever be reminded of this childhood nightmare. I know you are not lazy; you just need someone to give you specific instructions to get you moving.

This is where I can help you. Having learned to be organized, I can teach you techniques to get you started and keep you from giving up. That is what we do when we are overwhelmed with the system. I will not give you too much and you can work at your own pace. The best part is that when you are ready to take the next step, you will recognize your accomplishment and give yourself a much-needed pat on the back and proceed. We are not looking for perfection any longer; this is a process. One BabyStep at a time will set you on a flight path toward the home and life you have been yearning for.

BabySteps, BabySteps, BabySteps

Like anyone, I also know you have tried very hard to overcome your chaos and clutter. And, likely, you've tried more than once or twice. In the past when you have purchased a new book on home organization, you have jumped out of the starting gate at a full sprint, only to crash and burn two days into the system.

You cannot run before you walk! Think about infants building strength in their arms and legs by scooting around on the floor. Then before you know it, they begin to crawl, and soon they are pulling up and attempting their first BabyStep. They have their parent close by, but they really can't teach them how to walk. It is a process of getting up and falling down. Each time they stand they are exercising the muscles that will eventually have them toddling around the house.

This is how I see you! You are all my babies, my little FlyBabies learning to take BabySteps that will eventually have you FLYing!

When you catch yourself wanting to jump ahead, I want you to think about learning to walk and be satisfied with your BabySteps! When you start wanting to see the whole picture, you will miss the most important part of the system: Practice and reinforcement of your small do-able routines.

As you establish these new habits and begin to build the foundation of your routines, you are going to be so surprised at the ease with which you can add new habits to your basic routine. I don't expect you to run with these ideas and have a full-blown routine the day after opening this book. It took me nine months to develop my complete routine and it is still being nurtured. So, as it takes a baby nine months to grow in its mother's womb, you are going to see gradual changes in yourself and in your family.

Don't expect changes in a few days. This is not a book on how to control your messy children or your spouse; this is all about you, your attitude toward your family and yourself. You are not going to like everything I tell you about yourself and you are not going to enjoy some of the things I tell you to do. But step out in faith because you are looking for something different. Besides, what you have been doing has obviously not been working, so what have you got to lose? At the worst you will put this book on the shelf along with those dozens of others collecting dust. But, on the other hand, if you follow my BabySteps, eventually you will give all of those books away because this is the last book you will ever need in home organization.

What have you got to lose? CHAOS!

Psychologists say that it takes 21 days to establish a new habit. My experience is that it actually takes us 27 days for this habit to become a way of life because we are bound to forget and have to start counting all over again. Well not with this system you don't. All you have to do is continue to tally up the days you have done it and pat yourself on the back for a job well done. We will no longer throw the baby out with the bath water. I am so proud of every step you make and as you take them, you will be, too.

All our lives we have been put down by our family and friends, but the absolute hardest person on you is YOU! From this moment on, you are going to be your biggest cheerleader. Look at the cover of the book. Do you see the cartoon of FlyLady? When I was describing what FlyLady does to the cartoonist, we told him FlyLady was a cross between a fairy Godmother and a cheerleader with a drill sergeant personality. He pegged FlyLady on the mark!

As you go through your BabySteps to a new way of thinking you are gradually beginning to love yourself. It is this lack of self-love that keeps us from being all that we want. I know that this is hard for you to understand right this minute, but follow what I say and over time, you will see the reflection of yourself all over your home.

"Clutter attracts clutter!"

Dear FlyLady...

CLUTTER STEALS YOUR MONEY!!!

Clutter steals my money in so many ways!!! Just today we had to go buy another spreader for the lawn. Why??? Because we can't "find" the one we bought last year under the pile of clutter in the garage and the other one we own was ruined by a bunch of paint which was spilled all over everything. That is just one item … I can't tell you how many garden hoses, lawn mowers, rakes, sprinklers, etc. that will have to be replaced this year due to clutter.

My hobby room is a disaster. I know I have already bought the same piece for a scrapbook page twice but since I can't find it on my table, I'll end up buying the 3rd one this week …

It's Easter tomorrow and I'll end up buying new shoes for my girls tonight because we can't find one of each pair they already own … too much clutter in their closet!!

Clutter steals not only my money, but my sanity!!!!

Nothing gets done because I waste my time having to go buy more to replace what I can't find … adding to the problem.

You, dear Flylady, are helping to pull me out of this fast spiral. Thank you!

Lysa from Kansas City, Missouri

Your Second BabyStep—
You Can't Organize Clutter

Remember this new term: **Hot Spots**. They are something every home has — and in this chapter we'll talk about them and about other important tools for conquering clutter. The main goal of this chapter, however, is to learn decluttering in a way that takes you only 15 minutes a day.

Now, are you dressed, in shoes, with your hair and face fixed? If you answered "Yes!," I AM SO VERY PROUD OF YOU! If you have not yet done this, go do it now! This is a prerequisite for the next steps.

Let's Evict Your Clutter!!!

Few people think clutter is good — but do you ever think of just how much it **really** affects your life? After you read the following pages you will never walk into a cluttered room and feel the same.

We have developed solutions to your clutter problem. Let's start with the obvious. The Oxford English Dictionary defines clutter as "a crowded and untidy collection of things." That's a very sterile way to look at this truly evil problem.

Consider clutter in these ways:

Clutter is too much in too small a place. There are many of us that have too much stuff in homes that are too small to hold it all. This happens for many reasons: Your family has expanded while the size of your home has not. You have brought too much stuff into a home that was never big enough in the first place.

Do you move or do you try to streamline your "stuff"? How many of you have tried to use plastic totes, nifty storage boxes, little rolling carts, and laundry baskets to organize things? I will let you in on a little secret: *"Clutter can't be organized!!!!"*

When you have too much stuff in too small a space your home can't breathe, you can't breathe, the clutter will take over, and you will feel smothered in your own home.

Clutter is things that do not bring you joy, you do not love, or you don't need. Things that you use, love, and enjoy are necessary and important to have. Things that you have in your home that you don't need or don't like will have the opposite effect on you: they will make you feel negative and dragged down.

Clutter is disorganized. You may have things that you love and things that bring you joy, but if they are just stuck everywhere and have no real order to them, they will still have the same negative effect. You may have a beautiful collection of antiques but if they are everywhere, covered in dust, with no sense of flow, then you are not really enjoying them to their full potential.

Clutter can keep you living in the past, or reliving the past. When you have things around you that don't bring you joy from your past, you can't move forward.

Clutter causes problems in your family; I don't even think I have to explain this one.

Clutter makes you feel embarrassed and ashamed. How many times have you turned people away or not invited people to your home because of the clutter?

Clutter has a way of taking over our lives before we even know it. Clutter becomes that unwanted houseguest that you can't get rid of. It robs us of peace while we are home and it also steals any bit of joy when we leave home. Worse, it creates a feeling of dread when you know you have to return to that mess. How many times have you stayed late at work just to avoid the clutter in your home? What about those of you that will not go anywhere because of the chaotic state of your home?

Clutter has to be conquered. Don't think so? Look at some of the things we give up so we can devote our lives to this selfish houseguest. I received a message once from a lady who gave up her family vacation to clean and declutter their home for the safety of a crawling baby.

"Release your clutter and find the things you are searching for."

Clutter-filled homes are not welcoming to friends or family. So we do not invite them over often. When we do, we almost kill ourselves trying to get the house presentable so we will not be embarrassed. You know the drill. Major Crisis Cleaning until 3:00 AM because they are coming the next day. As a result of not wanting to make the preparations, we alienate ourselves from our friends and family by closing our doors and throwing away the key.

Clutter does not allow your mind and body to rest. The guilt of all the clutter keeps you working non-stop. You can't organize clutter; you can only get rid of it, like a cancerous tumor. Purge it from your life and you will find out what living is all about.

Not convinced? Here are more thoughts to ponder:

Clutter causes you to turn down invitations to lunch or weekend getaways with your husband. It will also get in the way of you taking time for you. It yells at you, "You don't deserve to have any fun; you have not taken care of ME yet!" Oh, selfish clutter. Like a spoiled child, it requires all of your attention.

Clutter also sends a subconscious message. Clutter tells the world that you are not worthy. We have all heard it. If you can't take care of this, you can't have anything else. We have been brainwashed by this clutter to believe that we do not deserve to have nice things, since we can't keep our home looking presentable. So we buy more clutter at yard sales and junk shops because it only costs a dollar.

Now don't fuss about this. I love yard sales as much as the next person, but think about this mentality for a few minutes. Don't we deserve to be surrounded by pretty things that we love, instead of someone else's cast-offs? When we quit wasting our money on more clutter to feed the already growing demon in our home, we can save to purchase things that make us smile.

Clutter never wants you to leave home. This is why it makes it so difficult for you to pack and go on vacation. Laundry has to be done; you have to get people to come to the house to feed your critters or, worse yet, you need someone to house sit for you. Clutter will never allow strangers in its domain. It wants you all to itself. The bills have to be paid. Before you can go, clutter invades your finances and family responsibilities. You don't have wills done because it is just too much trouble. You stay home, so you won't have to make the decision of who will care for your children in case of an accident.

Clutter loves to make you sick. Clutter attracts dust which then can affect your health. How many of you suffer from headaches, sinus problems, and allergies? This way you are totally dependent upon its way of life. It robs you of your health, so this gives you an excuse to give it more clutter. The more there is the happier it becomes and the sicker you get. Sometimes you will not allow people to come into your home to help because clutter has quarantined you. Or shall we say imprisoned you in your dungeon?

Here is yet another way to see clutter:

Clutter is to our homes as cholesterol is to our arteries. This is scary, so let's examine the similarities:

- Cholesterol clogs arteries. Clutter invades the pathways of our homes.
- Cholesterol increases blood pressure. Clutter causes stress in your life.
- Cholesterol reduces your life span. Clutter decreases your joy in living.
- Cholesterol costs major money when you treat it. Clutter pushes money away from you.
- Cholesterol causes heart disease. Clutter destroys closeness in families.
- Cholesterol is a result of over-indulging in fatty foods. Clutter is a result of over-indulging in stuff.
- Cholesterol causes arteries to harden. Clutter causes hearts to harden.

Do you see that we have to put our homes on a cholesterol-free, clutter-free diet?

How do we do this? By changing our "eating" (acquiring) habits. We live in a society in which the one who dies with the most stuff wins! Do you want your stuff to be the death of you?

Start changing your habits by only buying things that are needed.

Clutter was clogging up my pathways to abundance. When I got rid of my clutter I opened my heart to all the joy that life has to offer.

Clutter's main sustenance is chaos. When you are running around your home searching for something in all the mess, clutter is celebrating with a feast. Trying to find a document on your desk is not fun for you, but clutter begets clutter. You end up making an even bigger mess during the search.

The answer is no more clutter!

Your life will work better when you know where things are. You will be more productive. How many of you lose your house keys on a regular basis? I used to! Now I make sure that I have a specific place for them and use it! I had to train myself—and I rarely lose my keys anymore!! Things that are disorganized are things that don't have a proper place or that have strayed from where you usually keep them: Mail, keys, pens, pencils, calculators, scissors, shoes, books, etc. These become your Hot Spots!! (see p. 30)

Clutter loves ignorance, because you know no other way to live. If you did, clutter would not have a home that provides it with all the undivided attention that you give it. You have never enjoyed a peaceful afternoon without clutter vying for your every thought and deed. It knows that if you ever feel one ounce of peace, you will tell it to hit the road, because that peace is so contagious.

So, enough already! How do you get rid of this most unwanted houseguest?

It is not easy. It keeps pleading, "You need me" and laying guilt trips on you for what relatives will think if you put it out into the cold. (You know those gifts and inherited clutter you have been saddled with over the years.)

Your clutter did not accumulate overnight and it is going to take days, weeks, and sometimes several months to rid yourself of this squatter. We do it in small steps to make it easy on you. This way, your houseguest has no clue that you are evicting it. Slowly but surely the clutter will leave when we use our 27 Fling Boogie or 5-Minute Room Rescue. (See pages 31 and 35.)

Some of you may need to take a "get tough" approach and order a Dumpster or set up regular pickups from charity thrift stores. Whatever you decide to do, consistency is the ticket to getting clutter to vacate your premises. Just 15 minutes a day is all you need to set it on the road. When you kick its bottom out your door, you will begin to have your home to yourself again. Peace is just a 27 Fling Boogie away.

BabyStep Tool Box For Dealing With Clutter

Do you have your shoes on and are you dressed, with your hair fixed and face gleaming? You cannot attack clutter until you are dressed for the job and I don't mean frumpy sweats either. The work you are about to do does not require a safety jumpsuit or a hardhat.

The Old Way

I'll bet in the past clearing out a room was like this: sorting through piles and moving them from one place to another, never really getting rid of it for all time. As a result your clutter continued to pile up each time you brought home something new.

The New Way: Meet The Timer — your new best friend

We all dread cleaning because we think we have to do it all day. I make it fun by setting a time for short increments. Making it fun gets the job done! So get and set a simple kitchen or other sort of timer to five, ten, or fifteen minutes. You can do anything for fifteen minutes and it won't kill you.

Bring in the new, fling out the old!

1. Helpful Hint. Don't let it in to begin with. Every time you buy something new, take the bag or bags that they came in and pack up a similar item to give away. A born-organized friend taught me this. I watched her add a new pair of tennis shoes to her closet and cull out an old pair for the trash or charity. It made so much sense, why had I never thought of it? At the time I beat myself up over it; now, I realize that our minds do not work like this and it takes a good example to show us the way. You won't even realize you are removing the old. If you cannot find a similar item to dispose of, then you get to pick out two unrelated items to toss. This practice will help keep your home clutter-free before it even gets through the door.

2. The Famous 27 Fling Boogie

This is a fun, fast exercise! I practiced this daily for six months until everything in my home was something I loved and used regularly. In Suze Orman's various books, such as *The Courage to Be Rich*, she suggests a simple tool. I have adapted it because I was studying Feng Shui principles for putting order in my home.

Suze says take a garbage bag and run through the house collecting 25 items to throw in the trash. I took it two steps further. I added two items to the collection tally because of my interest in Feng Shui. This really doesn't matter, but it made it fun for me.

Now set the timer. In the beginning, you can start at 15 minutes. This will become your daily routine. Turn on the timer, grab a box, and go through your home as fast as you can, collecting things to give away. Speed is the key. Don't think about it and talk yourself out of tossing the clutter. As soon as you have the box filled with 27 items, take it immediately to your car to be disposed of at your local charity thrift shop. Stop when the timer goes off. That's enough for the first day.

You have done something for yourself and for someone else and you should feel so good about this. You will be blessed for giving your excess to those in need; you will also be blessed by getting the clutter out of your home, so you can find peace.

Now don't tease yourself into believing that you can have a yard sale and recoup your wasted money. There is no way that you are ever going to get back what you have spent, so forgive yourself for the waste and let it go to bless another family.

Be a songbird, too.

I have a favorite song that I sing at the top of my lungs when I am removing clutter from my home. It is a take-off on the old country music song, "Please Release Me, Let Me Go," as sung from two points of view. The first version is from my point of view or how the clutter is holding me back and won't allow me to live in peace. The next verse I sing from the stuff's point of view,

"If it doesn't make you smile, get rid of it."

29

begging to be released from a home that doesn't love it to a home that will use and love it. I don't know the words to the whole song, so I just make up new words each time I sing it. Tossing while singing helps you to FLY!

Do this every day until your clutter is gone.

The Next Clutter Control Method: Hot Spot Fire Drill

What is a **Hot Spot**? A Hot Spot is an area that, when left unattended, gradually and insidiously takes over your home. Think of a Hot Spot in a forest fire. It may seem under control but it really isn't. If left alone it will eventually get out of hand and burn up the whole forest.

This is what happens in our homes. If left unattended the Hot Spot will grow and take over the whole room as well as make the house look awful. When you walk into a room, a Hot Spot is the first thing you see. Your eye is locked on it. Over the years my Hot Spot has migrated. As a child it was a chair in my bedroom. I would pile it to the ceiling. It has been a corner filled with unopened storage boxes. Right now I have two Hot Spots in my home: a table by my chair and our big coffee table. This coffee table is a staging area for unopened mail. Sometimes you cannot see the top of the table.

Do you know why Hot Spots exist? It's simple. There is an unwritten rule of clutter. Clutter attracts more clutter — like a magnetic force. Whenever you catch yourself saying, "I can put this here and do it later," you have created a "Hot Spot."

You will know where your Hot Spots are because the rest of the family sees them as a place to put things when they do not want to put them where they belong. But you are going to put an end to this and stop this Hot Spot from becoming a raging "clutter inferno."

The Hot Spot Fire Drill

Twice a day, as a part of our Morning and Before Bed Routines, we will survey our usual Hot Spots and put away the items that have just been left out. If we take only five minutes to find a home for those items that are trying to take over, the Hot Spots will disappear. Easier said than done? Try this: in order to keep them from igniting, place a decorative object there or a vase of flowers, and you are going to be so pleased with your home as you put out the fires.

"Let go of the things that are holding you down and FLY!"

Time for the Five-Minute Room Rescue — another step on the road to clutter recovery.

Do you have rooms that you can't even walk through? I used to. In just a few short months, I rescued each of them from the CHAOS that had invaded by taking only five minutes at a time to put things away and toss things out. Keep in mind that this means purging the room of the clutter. You cannot organize clutter. Quit stepping over, on, and around this clutter. This room is not a landfill.

Garages and basements beware, you are about to be reclaimed for family fun! At one point all I could do was go in the room and put two things away or toss them in the trash. BabySteps will get you there.

Quick Review

If you do nothing else besides getting dressed to shoes and spending 15 minutes a day tossing out your clutter, you are going to see major changes in your home and the way you feel about yourself. This is all I ask. You can do this by setting a timer and spending the whole session in one area or you can spread it out over Hot Spot Fire Drills, Room Rescues, and 27 Fling Boogies.

Get the family involved and let the clutter fly out your door. Have fun and before you know it, you will be FLYing too.

Crisis Cleaning 101

In the event that you need to see some progress and you just can't seem to get into our BabyStep method, I have a tip or "gimmick" for you. Pretend that you are going to have guests or better yet actually invite someone to spend the weekend or have dinner one night. This puts the pressure on you to get your Franny moving.

Naturally, you will do the good old Crisis Cleaning, Stash and Dash. But this does allow you to begin to keep it clean with the foundation of your simple routines. After a few months of consistency, you will gradually be getting the hidden clutter disposed of while keeping the surface clutter at bay.

Many of you have written to us saying you work better from this starting point. I have even had members become cleaning partners, helping each other one day a week to eliminate the surface clutter.

Marathon Clean — if you really have to

I can hear the panic in your voices. "In six weeks I have a ton of company coming, what am I to do?" If you want a crash marathon cleaning session, I can help you, but be warned: without the routines, your home will be trashed again in a day. So you have to listen closely.

> *1. Go get dressed all the way to shoes, hair fixed, and face moisturized or makeup put on. Don't question me on this. Just do it now.* Put on some good working music. Not too fast, just slow and steady, peppy but not aerobic. Light a candle

that has a good scent or put some spices on to boil on a very low heat.

2. We are going to start in our kitchens. As the kitchen goes, so does the rest of the house. Set a timer and spend 15 minutes in the kitchen. If your sink is not clean and shiny, then shine it first. Then you can fill the sink up with hot soapy water and start to clear off the left and right counters. Empty the dishwasher. When the timer goes off, stop what you are doing and go to the living room.

3. Set the timer again and do 15 minutes cleaning off the coffee tables or picking up toys or newspapers. Concentrate on one thing, not all of it. Get a laundry basket and put the things that don't belong in the living room in the basket. Take a garbage bag with you as well. Start throwing away the trash. Don't get caught up in the guilt we have about pounds of trash going into a landfill. It is not going to kill you. Your home is not a landfill. So get over this perfectionist attitude. As you get your home in order there will be plenty of time to recycle. For now we are focusing on getting the home presentable. You can't do this if you are hyper focusing on sorting and recycling. When the timer goes off, go back to the kitchen.

4. In the kitchen set the timer for 15 more minutes and continue to work on clearing the counters. *Do not get sidetracked and begin to clean out a cabinet. We are doing only surface cleaning.*

5. Now take a break and walk around and look at what you have accomplished in just 45 minutes. Set the timer for 15 minutes and drink a cup of tea or coffee or whatever you love and just relax. When the timer goes off you are back in work mode for 15 more minutes.

6. This 15-minute session is in the bathroom. Do you understand this? Clean the sink in here first, then pick up towels and dirty clothes and put them in the hamper. Do not get sidetracked and start a load of laundry. I mean this. Laundry will come later!

7. When the timer goes off, you are back in the kitchen for 15 more minutes. We can do anything in 15 minutes. Keep working till the timer goes off. Then you go to the living room once again.

8. In the living room, continue to pick up and put away for another 15 minutes.

9. Every 45 minutes take a 15-minute break. Are you beginning to get a feel for this?

Adapt this schedule to fit your physical limitations and children's needs. But you get the picture. **Stay focused on one job for 15 minutes**. You are going to be so surprised at how much you get done in two hours time or spread out across the day with plenty of break time.

Now you can understand why the timer is your new best friend. You can do this if you have to. You have in the past, but have forgotten to take breaks and recharge your batteries and strategize. Your home will not stay this way unless you establish your routines, 5, 10, or 15 minutes at a time.

Tool Box Inventory Review

A timer

Bring in the new and fling out the old

27 Fling Boogie

Hot Spot fire drill

15-minute declutter sessions

5-minute room rescue

When all else fails, invite guests and Crisis Clean.

Homework Assignment:
Time For Another 27 Fling Boogie

Grab a garbage bag and boogie! Run through the house as fast as you can and dispose of 27 items. Then put the bag in the trash. Do not look through it. After you have thrown out the trash, pick up another bag or box and gather up 27 items to give away. Do this as fast as you can, don't think, just boogie. When you have filled the box with the 27 items, go take it to your car and put it in the trunk. Don't second-guess yourself! Next time you are out, donate it to a charity. You can do this. As you lighten your burden by giving away your excess, you will be free to FLY!

"By thinning out clutter, the real beauty of your home shines through!"

Dear FlyLady...

I have to tell you about a 27 Fling Boogie I had recently. I had in the back of my mind about the time we were asked to part with a cookbook. (BTW, I parted with at least 8 of them, and it was very freeing.) Anyway, I gave myself the challenge to look in my undies drawer and see if there wasn't one pair of undies I could throw away. I began my search and discovered bikinis that I had been saving "in case I'd want to wear them again someday." I'm 45 years old, so that is highly unlikely! So I stood there and flung undie after undie onto my bed, along with a few old bras. When I was done, I counted up my fling. There were EXACTLY 25 pairs of undies and 2 bras! I started laughing out loud because I was able to do a 27 Fling Boogie in just one drawer of my dresser!!! Thanks, FlyLady, for all you do! Sue from Wisconsin

DECLUTTERING TOGETHER

This morning, my DH [Dear Husband] picked up something from the bedroom floor and wanted to know where it belonged. Without thinking, I said if it blessed our home, I'd find a place for it and if it didn't, it belonged in the trash.

Now, he wanted an explanation. So, I told him your way of decluttering — doesn't matter if an item is good or not, but only if it blessed us and our home.

We ended up with a leaf bag full of stuff from our bedroom, and later in the afternoon another one from the basement!

It is like a lightbulb went on in his head, and he is rethinking things. He has always felt if it is "good" we should keep it. I think your home blessing is giving him permission to free himself of everything he really doesn't need!

Thank you. It is so much easier to declutter when both of us are in agreement.

Terri from Pennsylvania

Dear Marla and Kelly:

First of all, I want to tell you I've been a FlyBaby for almost two weeks now ... I love your service, I could kiss you for it! *lol* My mother (who used to be my *cleaning lady*, coming in and helping me clear pathways through my house and doing 3 hours worth of dishes, etc. ...) came in my house the other day and her jaw hit the floor! She couldn't believe the change!! (I immediately brought her to your website and she signed up, too. I can claim a convert! *lol*) I have to admit I went a little gung-ho at first, I just felt I needed the immediate gratification of a clean house and then the routines would be easy to follow because it would just be upkeep ... well, I know you caution about burn-out, but my babywings did the exact opposite! And it worked for me :) It has, however, led me to a different problem, one I'm hoping you can help me with ... when I get your reminders, I automatically want to jump to go and do it ... but the hot spot drills are very discouraging because (and this is wonderful for me!) I HAVE BEEN KEEPING MY HOT SPOTS CLEARED and picking up after myself constantly!! Yes, it's a wonderful thing, but I get these hot spot reminders and want to go and do SOMETHING, yet looking around, there is nothing to do! So what do you recommend a FlyBaby do when she has already done what you're reminding her of?

I know this must sound strange because just two weeks ago I was pulling my hair out by the roots and crying, *where do I start???* And now I am asking for more instructions because my house is clean. *lol* But that is just a testimonial to how incredible your service is ... I got my house sparkling and my sinks shining in two weeks, routines down-pat, and now I WANT MORE!!! *hugs to you for your life-changing e-mails!*
Leigh from Ontario, Canada

Dear FlyLady,

A couple of weeks ago, you posted a way for us to do marathon cleaning (for those of us who have to get this done in a hurry for one reason or another), using the timer. We work for three 15-minute segments then rest for 15 minutes, moving to another room when the timer goes off. I must tell you how wonderful that is for me! I have a hard time getting motivated, but work really well under pressure. Using this method, in two days I have 3 rooms 80% cleaned and decluttered! They will be finished tonight. My husband has been helping me, although he doesn't like the timer thing ... he goes along behind me and takes the stuff I have sorted out into piles or boxes, and puts them where they belong, saving me that step later. Amazing how fast this goes! Our daughter is also getting into the act. I tell her which box or bag an item goes into, and she puts it there. This is soooo exciting! I can't wait until my friend comes over tomorrow and tells me how wonderful things look! Four more days of this, then all I will have left is the computer room and the garage (my 2 dungeons) to declutter. Amazingly enough, I had a charity call today and ask if they could take a donation next week; I told them, "Of course! When will you be by? I'll leave it on the porch." That was a God Breeze!

I just wanted to thank you for giving all of us the tools to get ourselves organized. I had the motivation, but just didn't know where to start ... your e-mails gave me direction, and the permission to do it how it best suits my family. (i.e.: I still don't wear tie up shoes, because of a medical condition, but I do wear sandals around the house.) God has given you a gift ... thanks for sharing it with the rest of us!

Learning to FLY one step at a time,

Jennifer from Washington

WORLD PEACE THROUGH FLYING

Dear FlyLady,

Is this worthy of a testimonial?

DH was just passing my laptop and being very interested in my FlyLady Project, caught sight of this, and explained the Hebrew meaning of the number 27.

In Hebrew, numbers represent letters which, when put together, make up a word. The two that make up 27 translate to English as the following:

Spotless, Pure, Clean, Clear, Transparent, Lucid, Innocent, Perfect, and Fine!

Wow, what incentive to carry on with my 27 Fling Boogies!

Also, our house is so much more peaceful! I swear my head clears itself when I come down in the morning and see my shining marble counters and sparkling sink! And I know that DH's and the kid's lunches are all packed ready in the fridge!

I think the children are more peaceful and DH too! There is more laughter which means that the members of my household are taking this outside these walls and projecting it onto whoever they come in contact with. In turn, these positively affected people must pass it on to their contacts. And if we join up all the dots where FlyBabies and FlyChildren are, we can make a Peace Link. So can we bring World Peace through FLYING? I know it is definitely more peaceful in our turbulent neck of the woods!

With Love and Blessings to Dear FlyLady,
Shulamit from Jerusalem, Israel

Running on Empty

In the beginning of this book I mention that taking care of yourself first is so important — not just taking a shower, but also eating right, getting enough rest, and even drinking water. There's a lot more to this subject to discuss. And to be honest, you can practice all the FlyBaby techniques in Chapters Two & Three, but learning to pamper yourself will help you be more productive than you can imagine. Ladies, let's talk about this heart to heart.

A Little More Of My Story:

Sometimes I sound like a drill sergeant — set your timer, do the 27 Fling Boogies!! But remember why my heart goes out to you. I understand the pain and sadness you have felt because of your messy home and what it really represents about your life.

You may have picked up this book in your never-ending struggle to find the magic formula to fix your family and your home.

But, sweetie, the problem with your home has nothing to do with idleness on your part.

I hear what you hear over and over again — the reason your home is trashed is because of your laziness. Wrong! I know for a fact that I have never been lazy and I will wager the same about you. Your problem is that you don't know what to do first and when you decide on a course of action, you are continually spinning your wheels and unable to finish anything. By the end of the day you are exhausted, the house is still trashed, and you have accomplished nothing. I just wish I could give you a great big hug. I am going to help you fix this simple problem. Now I have tears in my eyes as I write this.

Does everyone else come first?

The truth is that you are so busy taking care of everyone else's needs that you forget that you have them, too. You are running on empty. There is nothing left for you. I want you to know that you are important to me. Each and every one of you is like my little birdie. I want to take you under my wings and teach you how to FLY! When you first read about getting dressed in the morning, fixing your hair and face, and lacing up those shoes, I know how you bad-mouthed my methods: what in the world does getting dressed and putting on shoes have to do with how my house looks? But I am living proof, and thousands of others will tell you what a profound effect this has had on their lives. Give me a chance to explain this a bit more. Let me tell you how I discovered this twelve years ago when I was depressed and needed to be hospitalized.

"You deserve to feel good and look good. Take a few extra moments a day to start this upward flight."

42

This was not a fun time in my life, but I am very thankful for all the bad things that have happened to me because they give me the resources to guide you. During the ten days I spent in the hospital, my roommates were given the assignment to give me a make-over. They fixed my stringy hair, put makeup on me, and dressed me in nice clothes instead of sweats. Then they made me put on real shoes and not the house slippers I had with me.

After the first make-over I was required to fix myself up every morning. There were twelve people in my group session and everyone had to describe the difference in my outward appearance from the first day as compared to the new me. Then they had to tell the difference in my attitude and body language. Every single person in the group said that I walked taller, no longer slouching, and I had a smile on my face. They continued to tell me that my eyes seemed brighter and I looked like I had a purpose for living. The truth was, when I checked myself into the hospital I did not have a reason for living. I was feeling like some of you do now. After a death in my family and my marriage falling apart, I felt hopeless. The sadness had taken over my being and I didn't even know what was happening to me. This one exercise gave me back myself; I was finally beginning to love me.

How many times do you forget to get dressed in the morning because things come up and you have to take care of them? Then the next time you look at the clock it is midafternoon and you are still in your pajamas. Those of you that work outside the home don't have a problem with getting dressed, but most of the time you are waiting till the last possible minute before you have to leave in the morning. As a result you are rushed and exhausted from running this never-ending race to get to work on time.

Again, it is not that you are lazy; you are getting things ready so you can get dressed. You have a blouse in the dryer or something has to be ironed. If you have children I don't have to mention the scavenger hunt for a pair of socks that match the shoes.

Running On Empty

What has happened in your life, just like it had in mine, was simple. I was running on empty. I was even out of fumes. The "car thing" is actually the right analogy for our situations. Stick with me here.

Did you know that you actually can fill up your car before it hits empty and you are running around on fumes? One common trait that many in our FlyLady community share is this: **We don't usually do anything until we HAVE TO!**

Does this sound familiar? You are driving to an appointment, work, or to pick up the children and notice that your fuel gauge is on the big "E" and you don't have time to stop and get gas because you are already running ten minutes late. Then your car starts sputtering and you run out of gas in the middle of a busy road.

Look at what this mind-set does to you and your family!
- At that moment, you are under tremendous stress and almost in tears. This is not good for your health.
- If you are running late for work, your reputation of being tardy has been validated once again.
- You have to make excuses. No one wants to hear the same old reasons for being late.
- Your children are waiting for you to pick them up. This is not good.
- Your appointment has to be cancelled and rescheduled. What a waste of the professional's time and yours.
- Now, what about your safety issue — the traffic and getting the gas to get you moving again?

- You are stranded in the middle of nowhere. What now?
- You have to call your husband or a friend to come and rescue you once again; what about the time they lose in their day because you didn't fill up when you had a chance?
- Getting help costs money.
- Your children are crying and you are at your wit's end.
- Then you start to cry. Are you sick and tired of living this way?

What can you do to stop this from ever happening again? Most of your life you have been running on empty. Empty of mind (no time to think). Empty of body (you don't take care of yourself by eating right). Empty of spirit (you are depressed and feel martyred).

You run until you can no longer keep going. Does this sound familiar? Then you crash and burn, get sick, or literally run out of gas.

Let's stick with the gas tank analogy. The answer to this problem is to create a routine like this one:

1. Notice when the fuel gauge is on half a tank, and then start looking for moments of time when you are not rushed to fill up.

2. Figure out how often you need to fill up and set a specific time of the week to do just that.

3. I keep a spare twenty-dollar bill in my car so I will always have the cash on hand to fill up when I get a chance. When you use it, you have to replace it the next time you have cash in hand.

4. I also like to fill up at pumps that let me use my credit card right at the pump. This keeps me from having to leave my vehicle; it also saves me time in the long run.

5. Connect filling up with car clean up. Every time you fill up, throw away your trash. Or every time you clean out and wash you car, you fill up. We have a car clean up challenge each Friday.

This is how your life stays off "Empty" and begins to come together!

When you stop letting your fuel gauge steal your time, safety, and sanity you will begin to find a small amount of peace in your life. Think about those little bits of time anywhere that you can rescue if you just do a little planning. I know that this is foreign to some of you, but we can learn. I was so proud of myself today; I filled up with a quarter of a tank left in my car. Try it sometime. It is so liberating.

Running On A Full Tank

You will get rid of this stress as you learn from the FlyLady system to work smarter and not make it so hard on yourself. I want you to learn HOW to be nice to you.

Here is how you take care of yourself. Remember, it's all in the BabySteps:

- Laying out your clothes at night is one simple way to get ready to greet your day without this kind of hassle first thing in the morning. Only wear clothes you feel good in.
- You know how I feel about a shiny sink. It gives you something to be proud of, a sense of accomplishment.
- I want you to feel this way when you walk into the bathroom and see yourself in the mirror: No longer are you going to be scared by morning hair and bags under your eyes. The face staring back at you is not going to look helpless and downtrodden.
- Dress to shoes and fix your hair and face, even if you just put on some moisturizer.
- Take a few extra minutes in the evening to pick out your clothes, and then get up in the morning before the regular flow of children and duties; just 15 minutes can allow you enough time to attend to your needs. Some of you still don't

believe me. For you skeptics, I want you to try this for
one week:

- Go to bed at a decent hour and get plenty of rest.
- Spend time doing things that make you happy.
- Don't save little treats for yourself for special occasions. You
  are special every day and deserve to feel that way.
- Eat good food and eat regularly.
- Drink plenty of water.
- Treat yourself with love. Don't say ugly,
  negative words to yourself.
- Wear your favorite jewelry often.
- Take bubble baths or long hot showers
  as rewards.
- As you are working, schedule breaks
  each hour.
- Grab a book and read just for fun.
- Take a walk and smell the roses.
- Buy yourself a bouquet of flowers when
  you are grocery shopping.
- Light a candle just because you enjoy it.
- Set the table with good dishes for everyday meals.

*"Set the example in love
and quit being
a martyr."*

These are all foreign to you right now, but as you begin to FLY,
they will become part of your daily life.

There are also other ways we can take care of our needs.

With this system I don't expect you to work from the break of
dawn until midnight. In fact, once your routines are in place, you
will hardly be doing any housework at all. My Morning Routine
takes me 20-30 minutes tops and that includes getting dressed.
Along with the evening routine, I spend less than three hours a week

"blessing" my home. An inner peace comes with the implementation of your routines. I want this for you, but I can't do it for you. You have to be willing to try something different.

Have you ever been on an airplane when the flight attendant tells you to put on your oxygen mask before helping your children? The mother in you wants to protect the children and your automatic reaction is to help them first. If you were to adjust their life support masks first, you could be robbing your babies of you. This is what you do every day when you don't take care of yourself. Not only are you stealing your babies' mother and your husband's wife, you are sucking the life right out of you.

I am FLYing with a Full Tank! How about you?

Dear FlyLady...

FLYING MEANS TAKING CARE OF YOURSELF

I agree wholeheartedly with the fact that we are robbing our family of ourselves. I am guilty of trying to do it all and do it by myself. My husband died 7 years ago when he was 31 and I had two babies to raise: 3 and 18 months old. I truly think I was running on empty for many years. I had my family and church family, but I didn't have any me time or a partner to discuss things with. For the people who complain about their spouses not helping out, be thankful that you have him. Set the example and he will notice and hopefully start helping. Even if all he does is help run your children to ball practice or piano, that is a big help.

I decided when my youngest started kindergarten it was time to do some things for me. I started exercising and going out to breakfast with a friend. I now limit my kids to one sport per season and they take piano once a week. I started college last January and I am working toward a degree. I joined the list a few months ago; I am still decluttering, but I look forward to the day when I am just doing the reminders. I want to encourage everyone to hang in there. We know our houses can be clean because of all the testimonials we read on this list. School starts for us tomorrow and I plan on getting back in a routine to free up more time for me.

Have a great Sunday!

FlyBaby S.

I'm Worth It

Dear FlyLady,

For years I have been collecting lovely lotions and potions for the bath. Not just small amounts, but a large shelf in my closet, and a cupboard in the bathroom! Since January 1, I have been using them up because I have been treating myself to a bubble bath — every night!

Not only that, but I now have time to read which I normally would not have. This bubble bath thing is really something good! The simple act of taking fifteen minutes for myself at the end of the day signals my brain that the day is done. I am much more relaxed!

I have one more week until it is officially a habit. I find myself looking forward to my bath every night now, and because I am using up my stash of stuff, I am also decluttering at the same time! My skin is not dry because I am using good lotions twice a day!

This one small thing has made such a difference. I would say it is right up there with formulating the routines that keep my house in top notch shape! Why did such a lovely luxury evade me for fifty years? I was "too tired," "my skin will dry out," "I shower in the morning." Well, I still shower in the morning because that is another luxury I will no longer ever go without! It clears your mind, and gets you prepared for the day. Also, it gives you something to do while the coffee is perking!

I think a lot of us put caring for ourselves too low on the priority list. We have been told at one point or another that we are selfish for spending time on ourselves, rather than time on our home and family. Well, no longer! I am converted. I will never, ever let my days become so full that I cannot do something nice for me, at least twice a day, and always involving water!

Thanks, FlyLady!

Linda from Winnipeg, Manitoba

Attitude Is Everything!

As you may have figured out by now, a lot of success with FlyLady depends on a single word: ATTITUDE. This is important for two reasons: You can set an example of love for your family and you will get the family involved in the program.

I want you to ask yourself this question: Do I act like a martyr? Think about this for a while and look hard:

- Do you complain that you are the only person that ever does anything around the house?
- Do you throw in the towel when you clean something up and then two hours later it is messed up again? Do you say, "Why do I even bother?"
- Do you pout when you can't get your children or your husband to do their fair share?
- Do you know what their fair share really is?
- Do you only clean when you are mad?

- Do you hear harsh words come from your mouth when delegating jobs?
- Do you find things to do outside the home that give you an excuse for not taking care of the house? (I can hear it now: "I have worked all day; I just don't feel like cleaning the kitchen.")
- If you cook, do you refuse to clean up afterward because you did your part?

I get e-mails every day asking, "How do I get my family to help?" My response to them is to set an example and quit being a martyr.

Do you think that this is pretty harsh? I don't. Your attitude about housework has got to change. It is your responsibility to nurture your family. I know this sounds backwards from the current way of thinking. But it's not.

In the previous chapters you have learned about taking care of yourself. I believe that if you bless your family with taking care of yourself and your home you will see a difference in their attitude as well.

How can you fuss about your children having a messy room when you can't walk in yours? How can you *"Laugh every day, even if it's at yourself!"* order your children to put their toys away when your crafting stuff has been sitting on the dining table for three weeks? You know where I am going with this. We cannot expect our children to do things that we don't do ourselves. You understand this, I know.

You have to practice what you preach. When they see you doing the things that you have only fussed about, they will start to follow you. You are the leader in your home; as you go, so does the rest of the house. Many of you have seen this work. Many families have jumped on the bandwagon and started to do their part to keep the house nice.

Your attitude makes all the difference. You hear me because you know that I am just like you, and I have found a way to overcome something we are going to talk about in another chapter—my natural tendency to become Sidetracked. This is something that two very smart ladies who have helped FlyLady call a Sidetracked Home Executive—or a SHE. They are Pam Young and Peggy Jones and their system is part of ours today, and they are my heroes. I make mistakes, but I tell you about them so you know that I am human and a Real SHE. I struggle just like every one of you.

Quit being a martyr! Do the things that need to be done to get your home in order. If your children are not doing their jobs around the house, then take the jobs back and do them yourself. I had one Mom that could not get her kitchen clean because her son would not empty the dishwasher when she asked him to. It was his job and she was not going to do it for him. I suggested that she take the job as hers and give him something else to do.

When the kitchen is clean it keeps the rest of the house in order. A messy kitchen is contagious to your home. This mom's stubbornness was affecting her ability to do her routines. The routines not being done were hurting the whole family, spiritually and physically. I am not saying that children should not be given chores around the house. Just don't let their ineffectiveness hurt you. Find out what jobs they like to do so they can find joy in their work for the time being. This will all come together. You will see! We are not after perfection on your part, so don't expect it from your children or spouse.

Think about this idea:

Have a family meeting tonight. I would like you to sit down with your family and apologize for not setting the proper example in the past for them. Tell them about your new routines and about FlyLady. Ask for their help in establishing your routines. Be honest! Kids love it when you are honest or even apologize. This lets them know that you are human. Tell them your goal of a chaos-free home and ask them for suggestions. Don't just lay down the law. I think you may be surprised to see their reactions.

*"**Your attitude** **determines your** **altitude**. How high do you want to fly?"*

Keep This Positive Attitude Going!

Make sure your routines are written out on a piece of paper, listed in the exact order that they need to be done. Do this, even if you have to use mine as an example until you can edit them to be your own. This is a start. I don't expect you to do everything on my list in the beginning; it is a goal. I keep my routines in a notebook that lives on my kitchen counter. **I call it my Control Journal and it is fully explained in Chapter Six**. It is just a pretty notebook that holds my routines. I also keep a dry-erase marker with my notebook so I can mark through each item that has been done. The routines are in sheet protectors. I just love to see a whole sheet of items marked through. I will describe my journal in detail in Chapter Six, but first take a look at how I have organized my own daily routines. Use this as a starting place for yourself, if you wish.

Here is my Before Bed Routine:

✓ Start "to do" list for tomorrow

✓ Check calendar for tomorrow's appointments

✓ Put drinking glasses in dishwasher

✓ Lay out clean dish cloths/shine your sink

✓ Put magazines away. Pick up and put away items in the living room

✓ Clean off dining table/make sure the kitchen is clean

✓ Open mail (if you have not done so)

✓ Put shoes in the closet

✓ Put clothes away/lay out clothes for tomorrow

✓ Wipe off daily sheets (my routines in my Control Journal)

✓ Take medications

✓ Brush teeth

✓ Clean face/moisturize

✓ Shout : TA-DA!!! And celebrate your accomplishments for the day

✓ Read for a while

✓ Snuggle with your sweetie

✓ Fall asleep with a smile on your face and in your heart

My Morning Routine

(which I do before leaving the house)

✓ Set a wake-up time

✓ Get up

✓ Make the bed

✓ Get dressed

✓ Brush teeth

✓ Clean sink

✓ Brush commode

✓ Put on makeup or moisturizer

✓ Fix hair

✓ Empty dishwasher

✓ Make coffee

✓ Thaw dinner/set table

✓ Feed dog, cat, birds, squirrels, and other critters

✓ Do a load of laundry

✓ Check calendar/make calls

✓ Reconcile checkbook, bring balance forward

✓ Look at and check calendar list from last night

✓ Pick up, put away, and hit Hot Spots

✓ Take medications and vitamins

✓ Eat breakfast and sit down for a few minutes

✓ Morning GIFT (god, imagination, focus, and thanksgiving) meditation

✓ Check e-mail

And always remember those shoes!

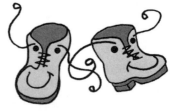

Dear FlyLady...

YOUR ATTITUDE AFFECTS YOUR FLYING

Dear FlyLady,

I wanted to share something with you. I've been following your system a long time and I finally realized something. When I stopped feeling like a martyr and started to serve my family, I had a big change in my life. Before, if the kids didn't put their dishes away in the dishwasher, I would call them in from whatever they were doing to put them away. I would get upset (but only in my mind, not verbally) when a mess was not cleaned up or my cleaning was disturbed, etc.

Well, just this last month I tried a new attitude. If there was a mess, I would say "Here DD [Dear Daughter], let me help you with that." If the kids had dishes in the family room, I would say, "I'll take those into the kitchen for you." My kids were astonished! They would say "Thanks Mom!" If my DH [Dear Husband] didn't put his dishes away, I didn't say anything about it, I just did it for him. I also started making my kids' meals again.

Usually in the summer I let them do their own thing. Well, I started dressing up their meals and snacks. I cut fruit into small pieces and put toothpicks in them. I added a piece of colorful dried fruit or candy to their plate. I served their drinks with ice and in fun cups.

Here's what's interesting: it doesn't take me long to make their snacks appealing. They like it! Okay, are you ready for the results I've seen in my home? First, my teenage DD hugs me with both arms and she squeezes me! I just love it!! She smiles at me a lot more and thanks me for the things I do for her. Both my DD and my DS are more apt to help me when I ask.

I told my DH that I really like us to have our meals together at the dinner table. He didn't say much but now he always eats at the dinner table rather than in front of the TV. My DH and I have started praying together at night. I asked him one night if we could and he agreed. We visit in bed at night rather than watch TV. These results are amazing to me! Now there may be a combination of things that have happened in our home but I really attribute a lot of the success to me serving my family willingly and not acting like a martyr.

Thank you, FlyLady! You are my hero!

Jodi from Utah

The Control Journal—
A System That Works
for Anybody

For many years I had a problem with not knowing how to properly use a planner or a calendar for appointments. I tried everything. Nothing ever worked until I started using routines. The problem was that I would forget to look at my calendar to see what was scheduled. Many of you are trying to figure out the same thing after missing doctors' appointments, meetings, and friends' birthdays.

This can be done a number of ways. I will teach you what I have learned through trial and error. Without my routines prompting me to look at my calendar, I still forget to check my appointments. So it doesn't matter what type of calendar or electronic planner you use. If you don't open it up, it will do you no good.

Each evening as I am doing my Before Bed Routine, I check to see what I have to do the next day so that I can lay out the correct clothing for the events. Do I need to dress up or are my denim jumpers O.K.? I do this as I am undressing and getting into a bath for Me Time. I also gather up anything I need for the meetings and put them in my briefcase or grab the briefcase I use for those meetings. (This is my solution to the many different boards that I belong to: a different tote bag for each, no more getting everything all mixed up!)

Then, the next morning, I get up and get dressed to shoes, hair and makeup as soon as my feet hit the floor. In the process of dressing I check my schedule again, just to make sure I am on track.

Before I became a County Commissioner, I could use a family wall calendar just fine. All I had to do was note my husband Robert's vacation days, as well as the days I had scheduled to teach a Fly Fishing class. Now I have many more items on my plate. I tried using a little pocket calendar. One trouble with that was I could not read my own writing, especially if I was in a hurry when I was writing it down. The other problem was that I would lose it because I did not have a specific place to keep it. **It was only when I put together my Control Journal that I was able to keep up with it.** The name Control Journal came from a dear friend that gave her zones nicknames, her kitchen was her Control Tower, just like an airport, and her journal stayed in her kitchen. So we call the system a Control Journal.

My first Control Journal was an 8.5 x 11-inch thin notebook in which I kept my routines. As it evolved, I became obsessive about this thing. I had tons of dividers and lots of paper; I even made a cover for it. Talk about obsessive/compulsive, I was a textbook case. The thing was so heavy that it hurt my shoulder to carry it, so I quit.

This is why I tell you not to worry about the Control Journal. It is just a notebook in which to keep your routines. I leave this part at home and only put my planner/Palm Pilot in my purse. I have found that I need phone numbers of business associates and family with me. If these are at home, I am out of luck.

The main thing you need in your Control Journal are your daily routines, your basic weekly plan, your zones/detailed cleaning list and your menus. Put all of these in sheet protectors so you can use dry erase markers to check things off. I will give you more information on this as we continue through your BabySteps which are explained fully in the next three chapters. As someone once said, "You don't have to see the top of the staircase to take the first steps." Do not feel that you have to put all of this together before you get started!

This will evolve as you establish your routines and practice your weekly plan and your zones. For now, just work on your Morning and Before Bed Routines described in the last chapter. If you need to adapt a little more to fit your family, you can add a noontime routine or an after-work routine. Whatever works best for you; make them fit you and your family!

"Our Morning and Before Bed Routines are just a simple way of taking care of things that need to be done each day. Our Basic Weekly Plan prepares us for next week. Our Zones keep us from allowing our homes to become overwhelming. It is all a process of thinking ahead, so you will not feel behind."

The second thing you will need is any kind of calendar, a wall one or a pocket one. Just keep it in your notebook or on the refrigerator so it is close at hand. The third thing you need is a notepad for making your to-do list and grocery list. Eventually you will have a place for all your addresses so you will not be searching all over the house when you want to send Aunt Harriet a birthday card. This can go in the back of your Control Journal, where you can write as big as you like, instead of in those little lines that are in the planners. We are always afraid of messing up the pages so we just don't write things down.

Now I have a Palm Pilot — and I love it! Before I got it, I had one of those really inexpensive Casio Digital Diaries. I used one of those for years. The only problem was my SHEness. I would lose all my addresses and phone numbers when I would forget to replace the batteries in the device. This happened three times. Of course, I had not backed it up with a written copy. So the copy in the back of your Control Journal can be your back up if you have an electronic diary. My Palm Pilot is hot-synced to my computer, too.

The Control Journal can also be a place for the family to find important numbers in times of emergencies. As my Granny always says, *Everything has a place and everything in its place.* Now don't start running around collecting all your family's addresses and start putting them in there. As you come across an address, put it in the notebook. Stick them in a zippered pouch or a pocket, and then on your desk day you can enter them on the sheet of paper. Use a pencil. This does not have to be perfect or pretty, just readable and in alphabetical order. This is why I ask you to have ABC dividers. Eventually you will have one main place for your addresses.

I hope this has helped to define the Control Journal for you.

Control Journal Supply List:

✓ A pretty notebook that looks good in your kitchen, or one with a place to slip in your own cover sheet or pretty picture from a magazine. It should have an inside pocket to hold a notepad, calendar, pen and marker. You probably have an old one around the house anyway.

✓ Several sheet protectors. Ten is a good number to start with. Don't get the non-glare type/matte finish because the markers don't erase as well. You may have to use a tiny bit of hand sanitizer on a Kleenex to get the marker off each night if you have this kind already.

✓ ABC dividers for addresses.

✓Colored paper. This is only because I love to color code things
like Pam and Peggy did in their book, *The Sidetracked Home
Executives*. Morning and Before Bed Routines are in yellow,
Basic Weekly Plans are blue, and I got a little obsessive and
color coded all my five zones. I used five colors:

Orange for the entrance, dining room and front porch
Yellow for the kitchen
Blue for bathrooms and other rooms
Green for master bedroom, master bath, and closet
Pink for living room and back porch

(You don't have to do this. I was just in an obsessive/compulsive
mode at the time. I do have my SHE obsession with color-coding and
office supplies.)

✓Blank dividers that you can label as needed: daily, weekly,
zones, menus, and grocery lists, addresses and emergency
phone numbers. And anything else you want to keep in your
Control Journal. Maybe you would like a section to keep
things that inspire you, or a place to put notes of the good
things that have happened in your life. Pam and Peggy call this
a Happiness File. I have one of written things in my Control
Journal and one in my e-mail files.

✓A pen and a dry erase marker in your favorite color. Mine
is purple.

✓A calendar or a pocket planner. It doesn't matter what you use
as long as you use it. You can keep your calendar in your
Control Journal, on a kitchen cabinet, or a wall close by so the
whole family has access to it.

But, in the long run, if you have not written your routines out on
paper, you don't need a notebook to put them in. What are you

waiting for, someone to do this for you? This one thing will help you more than anything else. Write down your routines; start small and practice doing them in the order you have them written. Make them yours, adapt to fit your family and be consistent in doing them each and every day. It is your recipe for Peace. The Control Journal is just a place to keep your routines. Use it and you will gain Control over your home and your life. Even family members will be able to see what needs to be done when you are out of town or sick. Seeing what you have done marked off will help them to realize how hard you really do work.

Have An Emergency Parachute For Your Control Journal

Every once in a while it is fun to just sleep in. Once, after my sweet darling husband, Robert, left for work at 6:30 AM, I hunkered back into bed to sleep for another hour. We were having a spring-time rain shower and it was perfect sleeping weather. NOT SO! You know how it is: you think that it is going to be restful sleep, and then you end up having bad dreams. My nightmare was just for you. It is going to seem like real life to some of you, so listen up! It could happen to you, too.

In my dream I started for the basement with a load of dirty clothes and it was flooded to the middle of the staircase. The lights were still on and I knew better than to go into the water. Now here is the scary part: I couldn't find any of my emergency phone numbers for Robert! By this time I was too panicked to even know what to do. I couldn't even remember how to turn off the power and the water. I was running around like my head was cut off. I didn't know whom to call first. Then I woke up and lay there for a moment and asked myself if I had those phone numbers listed in my Control Journal. I have Robert's work numbers in my Palm Pilot, but I had no back up in case it was not working and the computer was down.

Add this to your Control Journal:

Make a Tab or a Section for Emergency Contact

Get a sheet of paper and while you are calm, write down these emergency phone numbers in a way that everyone will understand. Put your name and address at the top of the page, along with written out directions so a babysitter will know your address if they have to tell emergency workers your location.

Call 911 if someone is hurt or there is a fire! If you don't have 911 in your area, then list the numbers of the police, poison control center, and fire departments. Now don't say to yourself, "Those are all in the front of the phone book." When was the last time you hunted 30 minutes for your phone book?!

List the names and phone numbers of your family doctors:

• Pediatrician
• Husband's doctor
• Wife's doctor
• Veterinarian

Spouse's emergency numbers, including cell phone and contact; your cell phone, and other phone emergency numbers, too. The babysitter could need them when you are gone.

Next of kin: your mother, father, sister, brother, or a close friend that lives nearby. List their names by their phone numbers.

Your children's school numbers.

Your insurance agent's phone number and claim number.

The emergency phone numbers for your local utilities:

• Gas
• Water
• Electricity

Now list your favorite, most dependable repairmen:

- Plumber
- Electrician
- Appliance repairman
- Carpenter
- Restoration company (one that comes in and cleans up smoke, fire and water damage.)

Now here is the tricky part!

Do you know how to turn off your water if you need to? Go look now behind the toilet and under the bathroom sink for a valve to shut it off. There is also a way to get into the plumbing for the bathtub or shower. It is usually in a closet behind a little door, but the closet is almost always piled to the ceiling. (Don't clean the closet out now!)

Could you turn off the water to the icemaker? There is usually a little valve under your sink attached to the main water line. It is not very big.

Do you know how to turn off your hot water heater? If it is electric, there will be a circuit breaker in the main electrical box.

Would you know how to turn off all the power to the house? There is a main circuit breaker in the same box. It is usually at the top of the panel.

Could you turn off the water to the house if you could not find valves for each water line? We have our own well water, so all I would have to do is turn off the power to the pump in the same circuit breaker panel. If you have city water, there is a meter at the street and it takes a special tool to turn it off. I bet you already have one. Find out where it is kept and how to use it. You will be glad you did. Just knowing calms you down.

What about the gas? If you have natural gas coming into your home, there is a valve that cuts it off too, but you should never even consider this until properly instructed by the gas company. I do know that if you live in an earthquake or hurricane area, you need to know how to turn this off.

Now I want you to look at what you have sitting on the floor. When there is a flood, the damage occurs from the floor to about your knees. What do you have stored in these areas that would be ruined by floodwaters? Is it stored in waterproof containers? Could it be placed on a higher shelf? Think about this. The sewer could back up into your basement (just like what happened to Kelly last year) or rising floodwaters could invade your home as many of our members have experienced in the past.

Take precautions now, so you will not be sorry later. It is much easier to FLY when you have a Parachute!

Chapter Review

Keep in mind that I don't expect you to set up a perfect Control Journal. This is a process and I have given you an overview. BabySteps, BabySteps, BabySteps. Purchase the needed materials for your journal and don't forget that this is just a notebook for keeping your routines in one place. It does not have to be put together before you can start this system. My routines are only an example for you. You are not expected to do a full-blown routine after just a few days of reading this book. Write down small routines, establish them, and then add to your simplified routines as you feel stronger. This way you will not crash and burn. You know you have thrown in the towel before because you tried to do too much, too soon and be perfect in the process. This is a trend. Progress, not perfection.

Dear FlyLady...

YOU ARE A QUEEN

Hello FlyLady and Team,

I have been a FlyBaby for about 9 months now and have wanted to write in for a long time. Finding your website has been a tremendous blessing in my life. I am a SHE to the core and have tried so many things to get myself organized. I am a SAHM with 2 fabulous daughters, ages 2 and almost 4. I am so blessed to stay home with my girls, and also my DH who telecommutes full time, but I have also felt like a failure for too long. My house was never clean enough, the laundry piled up the wall, the kitchen was so overwhelming and CHAOS was a way of life. A terrible way of life!!

Like many FlyBabies, I started out gung ho!! My kitchen sink sparkled, my clutter was under control and most importantly of all, I was no longer paralyzed by how overwhelming my chores seemed to be. Well, as the weeks and months went on (and we also moved away from all our family), I started to fall off the "FlyLady Wagon." But that was okay, because I had learned that it is all BabySteps and not feeling behind. When I would start to feel depressed, I would just take a peaceful moment and remind myself that the tasks were not impossible and that I could do it. I was capable. I believed in myself and have gotten back on track! For months I had never made a Control Journal. I really felt that was keeping me from really letting this system work in my life. One day a couple of weeks ago I turned my back on all of the things that were needing my attention around the house (except my family, of course!!) and took about 1 hour to put together my journal. That simple thing has made a huge difference. Having that list in front of me has really helped me to establish some better routines and not wander around the house wondering what it is I should be doing next. I just flip open my Control Journal and tackle the first item I see that is not checked off.

On another note, regarding the fact that we should feel like and be treated as queens, I totally agree. I have a tiara that I bought during Halloween for a few dollars and I wear it around the house while I am doing housework. (One time I forgot I had it on and wore it to the grocery store! LOL!!) I love the way I feel when I wear my tiara! I will stand up from wiping down a toilet and look in the mirror and instead of seeing a frumpy ole housewife, I see a queen!! I see a woman who has great worth. I want my daughters to believe they are growing up in a royal family, because they are!!

FlyLady, thank you from the bottom of my heart for helping me to see the queen in me!

Happy Holidays and God Bless America,
Queen Laura from California

7
Dancing Through Your Daily Routines

By now you know that we are called "FlyLady" quite by accident. It was my online nickname because I am a Fly Fishing instructor. And it just sort of stuck. But one day a God Breeze gave the name a whole new meaning! Lynda, one of our members on our e-mail mentoring group, came up with the acronym for FlyLady and it blew me away. **As you all know by now, FLY means Finally Loving Yourself. Let me tell you why it was so perfect.**

Ten years ago I started to practice something. At first just in words to myself while I would meditate. I didn't have a "mantra." I didn't even know what that was and didn't care. Still, somehow I knew I needed some words to help me focus. I chose "I love myself!"

As I would breathe in, I would say, *I love,* and as I would breathe out, I would say, *myself.* I would say it over and over. Eventually, each time I would close my eyes, those words would pop into my head.

Soon I was doing things to love myself. Getting my rest, taking bubble baths, reading books I enjoyed, spending time with friends that uplifted me, getting dressed every day and putting on makeup. By this time I was able to look into the mirror and not look away or find fault with my face. I loved myself with word and deed.

This is a major reason why this book is about so much more than simply removing clutter from your home and your life. If we do nothing else, I hope we impress upon you that if you don't take care of yourself, you will have nothing left to nurture your family. You will be filling their cups with an empty pitcher. Everyone will be left unfulfilled. You have found this book because you were searching for something, anything, to help you get your home in order.

The truth is, "Dorothy," you have had the power inside yourself all of this time. Your journey home is almost complete. Only a few more steps in your ruby slippers (routines and shoes) and you will find the peace you have been searching for your whole life. I know this sounds too simple to be true, but I promise that if you take care of yourself first, the house will come together like magic before your very eyes. If you don't believe me, then try to prove me wrong. Put down those excuses that have led you down the wrong path and focus on your goal. Use this system to guide you to your special place of peace. You will find it. Come FLY with me. I love you all.

Routines 101: here are the simple steps

Using the FlyLady approach of adopting routines, you do the same little jobs over and over every single day. This is not as monotonous as it sounds. I promise.

SHEs are very creative people. We hate structure because we feel that it bogs us down. Doing routines solves this problem. They free up our creative minds to think about other things because our bodies are doing the daily rituals of our home blessing: Routines! As you begin to train your muscles to do certain tasks one after another, you no longer have to strain to focus on what has to be done next. It becomes automatic.

My Morning Routine has become my time for praise and worship to start my day. I put on my favorite uplifting spiritual music and fill my soul with thoughts of my Holy Father and bless my family by doing my daily routine/ritual all at the same time. When you look at your routines as a blessing on you and your family, you are doing God's will. I do not believe that we can separate the two.

Now don't fuss that I am not worshiping my Father by mixing the two, because you are not going to change my mind. Putting my heart and soul into focusing on God and multitasking is a good thing.

This is when I get many of my God Breezes. My mind is open to His loving guidance and I am continually amazed by the essays that He gives me. FlyLady members tell me about them all the time in testimonials and comments. By spending this time doing my routines, thinking about God and listening to wonderful spirit-filled music, I am able to let go and let God mold me into all He wants me to be.

When your routines become so automatic, then you don't have to think about them and you can put your mind on things of the spiritual realm. There is no better way to get a blessed day started.

Start Small

If you are having a problem with your routines not becoming automatic, they are too big. This is why FlyLady's routines developed the way they did. I had to start with one item to focus on: shining my kitchen sink. Then I added getting dressed to shoes, and then, while I was getting dressed, I started swishing and swiping my bathroom. All of this only takes a few short minutes if you incorporate them while you are getting dressed. **Right away is the easy way**. Do it while you are there and then you don't have to think about it the rest of the day. Believe me, I have more productive things to do than go back and clean a bathroom.

This is not rocket science either: just wipe down the sink and counters, put away the toiletries, take a toilet bowl brush and swish it around the toilet once for good measure (without cleaner) and wipe up little boy messes on the floor. Most of this can be done with a dirty towel that is left lying on the floor anyway. You don't even have to use cleanser or paper towels — just a little bit of water will do fine. Then dry off the sink and the counter and toss the towel in the dirty clothes hamper.

If you have children, you may want to use a disinfectant spray on the surfaces they touch. Do that at least once a week. Now don't get picky on me because you have not been doing any of this and your bathroom has never been company ready. I dislike this term, because we should treat our family better than we treat company.

Once I am dressed, I grab a basket of laundry (if one looks close to being a load) and toss it in the washer. When I walk out of my bedroom, my bed is made. I do this as soon as my feet hit the floor! The bathrooms are clean. I purposely get dressed in both bathrooms so I can touch them up daily. As I leave our bedroom, I always turn around and check out how beautiful and peaceful it feels and then I smile and pat myself on the back.

Then I go to the kitchen, unload the dishwasher if it needs it and start thinking about my day. My music has already built me up in spirit and now I am ready to take care of me. I eat my breakfast, take notes on my God Breezes, and check my calendar for appointments.

All of this takes 20-30 minutes tops. If I need to take a bath in the morning, it will take 30 minutes. This whole time is so automatic that I just glide through my Morning Routine/ritual and enjoy every minute. You see, it is not drudgery to me; it is worship.

If you have never looked upon this time as a way to commune with God, you are missing out on a great time to renew your spirit and fill your soul with His love, all the while blessing your family and doing His will. FLYing is so easy when you start your day on the right foot.

Don't Give Up: BabySteps work!

I have been preaching BabySteps. Many of you want to see results much faster than using the BabySteps. This is our "all or nothing attitude" and our "Perfectionism"!

When we establish the small steps that comprise our routines, we will eventually be able to glide through them without even thinking. This is how my routine works. I do one job and this leads to the next one, until I have completed the chores that are needed. Before I know it, my home looks great and I am ready to have some real fun.

Think of it as dancing or driving. You don't consciously think about what to do next, it just happens. But until you learn the steps, you have to practice. We are practicing our steps right now. This is why I like you to put up reminders in your home so you won't forget where you are in the routine. So list those steps, even if you can't do them all right now. They will be your road map to the new life of automatic routines.

The Rhythm of Your Routines: another approach

While talking with a friend from Oregon, her words triggered a God Breeze for me. I asked her if I could use it for an essay and she agreed. Have you ever tried to learn a new dance step (not me, I have two left feet) or an aerobic workout? (I once won an award for being the most improved aerobically challenged person in our class.) Actually, the same process works when you learn a golf swing or

75

"Get your routines established one habit at a time."

how to cast a fly rod. The first time you do it, things just don't feel right. The muscles in your arms and legs don't go where you think they should. But the problem isn't with the muscles in your arms and legs, it is with the muscle that is between your ears.

Your brain is what works those muscles. If you don't have the movement choreographed in your head, your limbs will not follow because you have not given them the directions. One time I learned a fly-fishing distance casting technique in the rain, riding in a car. Once I put every movement into place in my mind, my arms and legs were happy to follow through. I got out of the car and performed it without a flaw. I had practiced it over and over in the car. I had developed a rhythm and the rest of it flowed into place. The result is what many people call "muscle memory."

This is why I don't want you to try to do a full-blown routine to start with. BabySteps and small routines will reinforce your routine rhythm and your dance will glide you along through your daily rounds. Do you see how adding new steps, as the first items become automatic, will help your rhythm? You will have confidence in the part you know and adding a new portion does not seem so difficult.

This is exactly how I established my routines — one habit at a time. You can do this, too. I don't want you to stumble and fall because you don't have the dance steps down-pat. Practice and having your steps written out on paper will help you more than anything. Decide which steps are your lead steps: is it keeping your sink clean and shiny? Getting dressed with SHOES, brushed hair and clean face in the morning? Laying out your clothes before you go to bed?

Then, as these become automatic, add swishing and swiping the bathroom and other items, one at a time. BabySteps are the key. You have tried the all-or-nothing system and it does not work. If you do too much too fast in order to see immediate results, then it's a guaranteed crash and burn. You will think you have failed again. I don't want you to fail. I want you to have what I have, peace, and this peace comes by practicing the steps to a routine, like mine. Now I glide through my day and the rhythm of my routines keeps me dancing to my FLYing Music. Put on your dancing shoes and come FLY with me.

Flight Check Summary:

✓ It takes 27 days to establish a new habit. I want you to figure out how many days you have been practicing your routines.

✓ Are they becoming automatic?

✓ Are you keeping them very simple? Concentrate on just a few items and as they become easier, you can practice other items.

✓ Do you have your routines written out on paper?

✓ Do you check things off after you do them?

✓ How is your attitude toward yourself and your family? Are you being nice?

✓ Are you giving yourself pats on the back?

✓ Are you taking care of yourself by getting plenty of rest, eating properly, and taking leisurely walks?

✓ Have you scheduled breaks for yourself?

✓ Are you taking your bubble baths regularly?

✓ Keep this in mind! You are never behind. You are not competing with anyone. This system is here to help you. BabySteps, Babysteps, BabySteps!

Dear FlyLady...

FLYING IN THE FACE OF TRAGEDY

I have been a list subscriber for a while, and wanted to share my story.

My husband is a marine stationed at the Pentagon.

He was at his desk on Tuesday morning in the A ring of the wedge that was hit by the plane. When I saw the Pentagon news report, I knew he was in that area, and spent two difficult hours waiting to hear from him.

He is alive and well.

Oddly enough, I found great comfort in the routines. I'm a home-schooling mom, and though I cancelled school for the day, I pulled out my mop bucket and mopped the kitchen floor and did dishes and bathrooms steadily. We have new neighbors, and their telephone and TV were not yet hooked up, so they were in my living room, which was nice and tidy, watching the news.

I kept my children away from the TV, but my six-year-old son saw the building on the news and said, "Mommy, that's Daddy's office building. Something awful has happened."

I agreed. Then he asked me if his Daddy was hurt. At that time, I had not yet heard, but this was my answer.

"Daddy is still Daddy, God is still God, and God is still in control. Even if something terrible happens, we'll be OK because God is still in control." He accepted that. And the sight of Mommy continuing her normal cleaning schedule, while he and our other sons played, seemed to give him great comfort. Thanks bunches for teaching me to have regular routines.
Amy from Washington, D.C.

RELEASE THE GUILT

I know that this essay of yours was about how we talk to our family, but the God Breeze that carried on this message was an entirely different one for me. Make one little change from "This is no excuse for being ugly to your family" to "This is no excuse for being ugly to yourself."

I've reached the point in FlyBabyhood that the newness has worn off and some of the motivation and enthusiasm has worn off with it. I noticed that the LR isn't looking as tidy as it should and the laundry wasn't ironed and put away immediately. As a matter of fact, it is still folded in the basket waiting for the ironing board to come out of the closet. What makes it so hard to just get this done and out of the way are my own berating thoughts. These thoughts beat me down and make me feel depressed. I thought that the clutter depressed me, but it does not. It is the way I talk to myself when the clutter begins to take over that is causing the depressed mood. I've been ugly to myself.

So it is time to release the guilt I lay on myself! I've been sitting here turning my thoughts to more encouraging ones, telling myself how much better the house is these days and how quickly it can be brought to order now. I'm telling me that I have learned the tricks and tools to make the house lovely and get through daily tasks with ease. I am beautiful inside and want the outside environment to reflect that beauty.

I think I feel a decluttering session coming on. It is a beautiful morning for ironing. Later I'll celebrate my inner beauty being reflected in the shiny tabletops by baking something special, or maybe by arranging some cut flowers. Flying is easy when you are being beautiful to yourself!

Joann from New York

The cure for CHAOS

Dear FlyLady,

I moved out of my parents' house when I was 17, and have been responsible for my own housekeeping ever since. I am now 59 and long ago accepted the fact that I was too lazy/disorganized/uninterested/whatever to ever have a well-kept home. Three occasions caused me special humiliation, embarrassment and pain: the unexpected ringing of my doorbell, having workmen trooping through my house and (especially) having company come and stay overnight.

A friend pointed me to your list the first week of this month. I was doubtful that it would amount to anything, but after reading your morning and evening steps for beginners, I figured I could at least do those things. I cannot begin to describe or even explain the results.

Last week my husband answered the door and I heard him welcoming a neighbor to come in to use our phone. And the living room was clean & neat and the kitchen counter by the phone was, too. The sink was empty and shiny; the tile floor was clean. The cat's litter pan was sweet and there were no spills around the dog's dish.

The next day a pipe broke and a plumber made an emergency visit. The bathroom was squeaky clean (although I still flinched a bit when he rummaged under the sink).

And the day before yesterday an out-of-town cousin called to say she & a friend would be visiting her aunt in the area and could we get together either Friday or Saturday. Rather than putting her off as I would have done in the past, I invited the two to come for dinner and then stay the night. Instead of frantically cleaning before they got here, I only set out clean towels and asked DH to brush the dog.

Is my house perfect? No.

Is my house cleaner than it has ever been? Yes.

Do I find myself more relaxed? Yes.

Even if I cannot get beyond doing the morning/evening routines I will have achieved something that I never thought possible.

Thank you, thank you, thank you.

Barbara from Florida

"Once a habit is there it becomes a mind-set. You don't even realize you are cleaning!"

Your Basic Weekly Plan — Every Day Has a Purpose

Do you remember when you were a child singing the song about the days of the week? *"This is the way we wash our clothes, wash our clothes, wash our clothes, every Monday morning."* Just think about all your little friends singing and pretending to use a scrub board. Our grandmothers actually did this. They had a specific day of the week that would be assigned for certain jobs or errands. This is the simplest way to describe a basic weekly plan.

We have seven days in a week, and each day we can have a different focus. This does not mean that we spend the whole day working on that job; it is just a reminder that if today is Monday, then we are supposed to do a specific job. Each and every week we have a list of things that need to be accomplished.

As I began to develop my Basic Weekly Plan, I decided to look at what my needs were. I decided I needed a day to play. Yes, you heard me right! I wanted to have time for myself, even if it was only an hour or two to do things that gave me pleasure. Keeping

83

my marriage alive was also important to my mission, so I needed a special time for my Sweet Darling. Then there is keeping in touch with family and friends, so I needed a day for family fun.

As I continued to look at what else I needed to keep me going throughout the week, I decided I needed a day for Renewing My Spirit. My week actually starts with Renewing My Spirit. I chose Sunday for this, but you can choose any day you like. So I spend time building myself up with song, verse, and communing with God. I never do anything on this day that makes me feel bad. This is my day for happy, uplifting thoughts. You can fill your day with whatever you like: church, family get-togethers, or just quiet time alone. This is your day to Renew your Spirit, let your soul guide you and recharge those spiritual batteries.

FlyLady's Basic Weekly Plan

I want you to think about the things you need to do every week. Select which days you want to do these things, put it on your calendar for next week and stick to it. Make an appointment with yourself. Try it for one week. It may surprise you that your week can revolve around these appointments. This is what I do. With the Basic Weekly Plan, we decide on a day to do things and stick to it. I never knew how much this would help my lack of organization. Knowing that I do my shopping on Thursday, my cleaning on Monday, and my desk work on Friday allows me the freedom to schedule things according to

"Do you have some time planned this week just for you?"

the day. When you know what the day is, you know what has to be done. It is another way to be on auto-pilot.

Monday: Weekly Cleaning Chores (8:00am-9:00am)
The Importance of My Timer

Monday I do my weekly cleaning hour. Yes, I only spend one hour blessing our home. If the truth be told, I only spend 10 minutes a chore. When the timer goes off, I stop what I am doing and start on the next chore.

1. I set a timer for 10 minutes and change the sheets on our bed. I will finish making the bed, but I go really fast with the timer.

2. Then I set the timer for 10 more minutes and gather up all the trash in the house and put it in the trash can.

3. After this I dust the horizontal surfaces with a feather duster in one hand and a dust rag and polish in the other. Only spend 10 minutes. Then stop and do something else.

4. Now that I don't have a carpet, I sweep or dust mop my floors. This takes me only 10 minutes. After the timer rings, I stop. Next, I mop up the puppy toe prints on the floor and also mop the bathroom. I stop after 10 minutes.

5. You can vacuum the middles. This means just the traffic areas, not under the furniture. Do this as fast as you can.

6. Now I spend 10 minutes getting rid of the old magazines from our coffee table. This doesn't take 10 minutes so I usually work on my constant Hot Spot, the table beside my chair, too.

7. After this I put the finishing touches on the room. I take the window cleaner and clean the windows in my front door and back door, then I clean all the mirrors in the house. You know, all those toothpaste splatters and dental floss home runs. I spend 10 minutes tops.

The beauty of this system is that it gets the basics done, but it does not have to be done perfectly. If you work outside your home and have to leave the house in the morning, then do some of these chores in the morning and some in the evening. In three days you will have your weekly cleaning done. Quit trying to kill yourself doing weekly cleaning.

Even if you just "hit a lick at a snake," you have done more than you did last week. Besides, the more you get your home decluttered during **27 Fling Boogies** the easier this will become.

So promise me that you will not beat yourself up if you don't get the whole house done. It is okay. You will do more next week. That is how this system works.

"Housework done incorrectly still blesses your family."

It is the perfectionist in you that doesn't think it is clean unless you can see it all done at once. This attitude is what got your home in the bad shape that it is in now. Eventually your home will never look dirty. We are so used to only cleaning when the dirt and guilt are so bad that we can't stand to look at the mess one more minute. You are going to be so surprised with your newfound free time because with your routines you will feel like you are hardly cleaning at all.

HOUSEWORK DONE INCORRECTLY STILL BLESSES YOUR FAMILY!

It may not be done the way your Momma taught you, but it will be done. This will make your home shine and you will smile.

OFF WE GO: Here is Flylady's Very Own Basic Weekly Plan

Monday Is Weekly Home Blessing

- Laundry
- Home Blessing Hour
    - Cull/toss old magazines
    - Change sheets
    - Empty all the trash
    - Vacuum all rooms
    - Mop kitchen and bath
    - Clean mirrors and doors
    - Dust/polish furniture

Tuesday Is My Free Day

- Water and fertilize plants
- Spend 15 minutes in the current zone

Wednesday Is A Day To Spend At My Desk, Making Lists And Planning Next Week

- Remainder of weekly cleaning
- Make sure refrigerator is clean
- Write thank you notes
- Work on menus and grocery list for next week
- Balance checkbook before going shopping

Thursday Is Grocery And Errand Day

- Make sure menus are planned before you go shopping
- Check grocery list one last time before you walk out the door. Take your list with you
- Grocery Day
- Errand Day:
    - Library • Post office • Buy gifts, cards, and candles

Friday Is Paperwork, Bill Paying, And Miscellaneous Day

- Be romantic today!
- Get food from the freezer for next week
- File papers
- Write letters and cards
- Clean out purse
- Mend clothes and polish shoes
- Pet care (Flea and Heart Meds)
- Clean out car and check fluids
- Clean laundry room

Yeah! It's the weekend! Time for the weekend dance!
Have some fun!
— FlyLady

Friday is Date Night

Saturday is Family Fun Day

Sunday is Renew Your Spirit Day

"Make time
for your
personal
joys"

Dear FlyLady...

HOUSEWORK DONE INCORRECTLY STILL BLESSES MY FAMILY

Wow!! I have been a member for about 4-6 weeks and just finished my first home blessing! What a wonderful workout. My heart was pumping and I was sweating and having fun! Yes, FUN!!! I didn't freak out over the toys on the floor, I just used the vacuum to push them to the sides of the room! I had a wonderful sense of coloring outside the lines, something I never did as a child!! I had to fight myself while mopping the kitchen, there were stuck-on things not coming up with a quick swipe. But, in the end, I left them there!! Normally I leave the floor completely gross because I don't want to spend 45 minutes on my hands and knees to do a "proper" job. I kept repeating to myself that "housework done incorrectly still blesses [my] family." Best of all, it's 10:00 a.m. in England and my house is pretty clean, I've had a shower and feel great! Thanks a mint!! FlyBaby from the United Kingdom

DATING DOESN'T HAVE TO COST MONEY—BE CREATIVE

Dear FlyLady,

For our first six years of marriage my DH and I thought we could never afford a date or time alone together. Last year our marriage hit rock bottom. We never took the time to work on our marriage or make it a priority in our lives. With the Good Lord's help we are rebuilding our marriage and we have come a long way since last year.

One of the greatest benefits we have now is a great friend we share babysitting services with once a month so we both can have a date night. We have enough gas to drop the children off and then we head home to enjoy the peace of our home for a few hours. By the way these times are now even greater since I am not cleaning all day long so I can come home to a clean house. Making time to spend together will bless your children more than spending all your time with them and being stressed. Once again Thank you FlyLady for helping us all.

Dena from Ohio

Zones—You Never Have to "Spring Clean" Again

You may actually be shouting, "Yea! Right! I can get this house clean!" In the back of your mind, however, you may hear a little voice saying, "But it will only stay that way for an hour; you have got to be kidding!"

Now listen very closely: I will say this over and over again, *"Your home did not get dirty in a day and it is not going to get clean overnight."* I will continue to reinforce this message; I do not want you to crash and burn. Do you remember, as children, our mothers and grandmothers would go into spring-cleaning mode about once a year? The house would be torn to shambles in the disguise of spring-cleaning. There would be lots of yelling, at least in my house there was. Beds would be dismantled, curtains would be taken down and washed, baseboards and closets would be cleaned. By the end of the day, the army of children would be exhausted and your mother would look like she had been run over.

Now that you are grown you must promise to never put your children through this. And, guess what? You will accomplish just as much. I am going to give you a tool that will keep your home in such good order that you will never have to feel guilty about not spring cleaning again!

This tool is called Zone Cleaning. It is as simple as it sounds. We break our home into five areas. Each week we focus on that one area. We do our decluttering first, and, eventually, we will do our detailed cleaning. There are lists suggested below that you can modify in your own way.

Detailed cleaning may seem like another name for spring cleaning without the negative feelings that come with it. But it really isn't. It is cleaning in BabySteps so that in a few months' time you will have totally decluttered your home. Zone cleaning is the process of doing a little each day. All I ask is that you spend 15 minutes a day decluttering and that you spend it in a different zone each week.

In Chapter One I told you to go shine your sink, to clean it well and polish it until you could see your reflection in it, regardless of the pile of dishes you had in the sink. You set them out on the counter and did exactly what I asked. Since that time, have you had to do that again? No! Because it has not gotten that dirty. Each day you wipe it out or spray a bit of Windex in it and then it is done. It takes you only seconds, yet you still get to see your reflection in the sink. As you work through your home with these cleaning zones, you will begin to notice that your home is never at the point where you think, "I have got to get this mess cleaned up today, I can't stand it anymore." Hey, let's face it, it looks so good that you don't have to clean.

Do not fall into that trap. With the zone system, we will never see dirt again. This is such a blessing. No more dirt to make you feel guilty; no more dirt that will keep you from opening your home to friends. You can do this. It will not happen overnight, but in about three months of consistently doing your routines, Basic Weekly Plan, and your zones, you will have a home that is ready for company at all times.

But don't jump the gun by dividing your home into six or eight zones. The number of zones is also key to the system. Each and every home, whether large or small, has five zones:

- entrance / dining room / front porch
- kitchen
- bathroom / children's rooms / spare bedroom or office
- master bedroom / master bathroom
- living room / family room / den

These are the main living areas of your home.

Zone Cleaning: let's get started

If you look at your calendar you will notice that most of the time the days of the month spread over five weeks. This is how we determine what zone we are in.

	S	M	T	W	Th	F	S
Zone 1				1	2	3	4
Zone 2	5	6	7	8	9	10	11
Zone 3	12	13	14	15	16	17	18
Zone 4	19	20	21	22	23	24	25
Zone 5	26	27	28	29	30		

Zone One: Entrance

On the first day of the month, start in the entrance. For now, all you are expected to do is declutter. Do not start detailed cleaning until the clutter is under control. Make sure you understand this. Work in this zone, even if it's only a day, until Saturday. On Monday we start a new zone. Since some months we only have a few days in this zone, we put the entrance of our home in Zone One.

Along with the entrance we add the front porch and the dining room. Usually these are the first rooms you see when you enter your home. Keep these rooms in this zone; do not change this. Stick with the plan.

"The entrance to our home makes the first impression on our guests, our families, and ourselves."

Detailed Cleaning Lists (after you declutter)

ZONE 1: Entrance

Start at the ceiling and work your way down to the floor.

1. Clean cobwebs.
2. Dust window sills and front door.
3. Clean switch plate of hand prints and walls if needed.
4. Put plants in the shower and give them a good rinse. Let them sit there until you are finished.
5. Dust furniture.
6. Dust baseboards.
7. Straighten the coat closest.
8. Sweep, vacuum, or mop the floor.
9. Put back the plants. You would hate for you or your husband to walk into a jungle tomorrow morning!
10. Add your own personal touches to make it more welcoming.

ZONE 1: Dining Room

1. Clean the cobwebs.
2. Dust window sills.
3. Clean the windows.
4. Clean doors of china cabinet after you straighten dishes if they need doing. Dust cabinet.
5. Clean and straighten any drawers.

6. Clean off the top of the dining table and polish.

7. Rinse plants in the shower.

8. Dust the bottoms of the chairs.

9. Dust the baseboards.

10. Move furniture and vacuum underneath (except the china cabinet. I turned mine over one time. It was not funny.).

11. Add your own personal touches to the table (tablecloth, pretty bowl, flowers).

ZONE 1: Front Porch

1. Sweep down cobwebs and spider webs (in the summer I leave them. I feed spiders, too.).

2. Sweep off porch furniture.

3. Sweep the porch.

4. Throw away any dead plants.

5. Prune back unruly bushes from the entrance.

6. Re-pot planters (in summer).

7. Refill bird feeders.

8. Wipe off tables, banisters, and light fixtures.

9. Get rid of unwanted items.

10. Add your own personal touches to welcome friends and family (wreath, welcome mat, bell).

ZONE 2: Kitchen
The Heart of the Home

Did you know that your kitchen is the heart and soul of your home? Do you like your kitchen? What does your kitchen say about you? As you are decluttering your kitchen, really look at it and see what others see. This is the room of the house that is like operation central. It is where meals are prepared with your love; it is where a lot of conversations take place in families; it is the heartbeat of your home. A Born Organized person once told me: "My insides don't feel in order if my outsides aren't in order."

As I said earlier, it was the kitchen that started the ball rolling for me, specifically the sink. I shined the sink, and it snowballed from there to the counters being clean, the cabinets straight, and the refrigerator no longer filled with starter kits for science projects. This then took me into the dining room and other rooms of the house. But the key to my story is that I decluttered the heart of my house, which uncluttered my mind and allowed me to continue through the rest of my home. Be proud of your kitchen—there is a lot of unspoken love that comes from that room.

The kitchen is a major problem area for most of us and we always need a full seven days to work there. This is not about spending all day cleaning in the kitchen. All I expect is that you set a timer and spend 15 minutes each day doing one thing. Do not pull all the items out of the cabinets and drawers and expect to do this in 15 minutes.

Remember this important rule: Do not pull out more than you can put back in an hour. Also, do not start repainting your walls and refinishing your cabinets. We are not redecorating, even though after a few months you will feel like you live in a new home. For now we are just DE-CLUTTERING! We have a tendency to jump in with both feet and get paralyzed by the mountain of clutter we have pulled out. We are taking BabySteps while we are establishing new habits. Eventually all your clutter will be gone and you'll have a way to keep it clutter free for life.

If your kitchen is close to being condemned, it is time to get in there and start to reclaim it. This may seem very hard for you right this minute, but we are going to focus on only one little part at a time, not the whole big picture. This is what SHEs do. We can't see the forest for the trees. We are not going to deep-clean our stoves, pull everything out of the refrigerators, or clean our drawers and cabinets first. They have been messy for a very long time and can stay that way until we have gotten a handle on the worst of the dishes, pots and pans, clutter, and trash. Are you listening to me? If you did not comprehend what I said, stop and read this paragraph one more time.

1. We are going to start with our kitchen sinks. Take all the dirty dishes out of the sink and drain out the nasty water. Then we are going to do our Shiny Sink 101 techniques. This is so simple, and the instructions are on the website. Just keep in mind: I don't care how many dirty dishes you have piled on the counters or the stove top or hidden in the oven and dishwasher; we will get to those very shortly. All I want you to focus on is getting the sink shining. Then we can wash those dirty dishes one stack at a time. Now, get to work! Get out some clean dish towels and dishrags.
2. Next we are going to fill our sinks with hot soapy water. If your dishwasher is full of dirty dishes, start it running, even if you don't have dishwasher powder. I don't use much because I use my china, and my dishes come clean. Hot water is a great cleaning agent. We are going to wash the dishes on the counters, one sinkful at a time, and put them away so they don't pile up and get in the way of your work. Clean the counter on the opposite side so you can lay your clean dishes on a towel or drying rack. Wash, rinse, and then drain, dry, and put them away. Don't get caught up wanting to wash them all and then put them away later. We are going to finish what we start and take BabySteps to do it.
3. Now, if your dishes in the dishwasher have finished, put them away and put another load in. It may be time to put some fresh hot soapy water in your clean and shiny sink again. Put all the clean dishes away to make room for the ones that still need to be washed. Put more dirty dishes in the new dishwater and by this time you may have one counter that is just about cleared off. If not, move all the dirty dishes to one counter and take the dishrag and wipe down the cleared counter.
4. Next we are going to gather up all the trash in the kitchen. First you have to empty the garbage can so you will have a place to

put the trash. Now put a new garbage bag in the trash can and start placing pieces of trash in the bag. This is a 27 fling boogie for trash.

5. Now that you have cleaned off one counter, go to the next one. What is this?! You happen upon your biggest hot spot. This is where you pile all your mail and receipts. Don't get sidetracked opening up the mail. Throw away the obvious catalogs and junk mail and take the unopened mail to your desk. Don't get sucked into cleaning off your desk either; go right back to the kitchen. We are focusing on our kitchens this week, not our desk area. If your desk area is in your kitchen, you have to get it straightened up so you can at least find your bills to pay them.

6. Slowly your kitchen is starting to look a little better. By this time you have spent close to an hour cleaning, maybe an hour and a half. It is time to take a break. While you rest, I want you to get a pen and paper and make a list of what else needs to be done in your kitchen. Work clockwise around the room and you will soon have a good idea of the other things that are calling out to you. Set a timer and rest for 15 minutes.

7. Now we are going to clean off the dining table. Don't balk at me. I know it is piled high, but it is time you tackled this major hot spot once and for all. Now go get an empty laundry basket, set it on one of the dining chairs, and then get the garbage can. Pick up one thing at a time and either throw it away or put it in the basket to put in another part of the house. When the basket is full, make a delivery run and put everything away as fast as you can. Then come back and start again. Now when you take a break, you can sit at your lovely, clean dining table.

8. After you get the table cleared, you can take another break. Now we are going to look at your pantry and make a grocery list of the staples you need to prepare meals. You know, the basics. Milk, bread, flour, sugar, etc. This is just the start of your pantry list. So don't get carried away. BabySteps.

Now let's look at what is left to do and make a basic plan to get it done during this next week.

* The old food needs to be cleaned out of the refrigerator. We do this on Wednesday.
* The stove top needs to be wiped down, not deep-cleaned, just the surface grease; we will get to the grime later, once the dishwasher and the sink are empty.
* We need to keep the dining table empty except when we are having dinner, so now is the time to declare it a sacred place. No more clutter here.
* The floor needs to be swept and mopped. Not now, but Tuesday is a good day for this.
* There are drawers that need to be cleaned out and reorganized, but don't get carried away; we will do this one drawer at a time.
* The same thing for the cabinets; one cabinet at a time will be cleared out and purged of unwanted and unused stuff. You know, all those plastic Cool Whip containers.
* The door and drawer fronts will eventually be wiped down too, but not now; this can happen as your new habits are established and you keep running out of things to do. Don't say this will never happen, because it has happened to thousands of people. As their homes come together and get cleaner, they have more time to notice and clean those things that have not been a priority in years, or ever. When you are so stressed out about the daily things, you can't see the dirt on the walls, switch plate, or outside door.
* Your pantry needs to be organized so you can easily find the food you want to cook and can see what you need to buy from the grocery each week.
* Your kitchen window is splattered with watermarks from the sink. It needs to be shined too.

I do not expect you to do all of this in one day; this is just a full out-line of what needs to be done, and in the next 3 months you will get around to it. For now, focus on getting all the dishes washed and put away, as well as on keeping them done each and every day. Keep your dining table clear so you will have no excuse for not hav-ing a family sit-down dinner. One good way to ensure that you do not trash the dining table again is to put a centerpiece on the table or a pretty tablecloth on it. You would be so surprised at how this helps to keep it looking nice.

Now it is time to give you some tips for keeping your kitchen look-ing nice and making it a place that is conducive to cooking, teach-ing, living, and loving your family.

* Keep your kitchen sink empty and shining.
* Make a grocery list each week before you go grocery shop-ping of the favorite things your family likes to eat. Always keep those foods on hand in the pantry or the freezer.
* Each morning think about what you are going to fix for din-ner. This keeps you from going into a panic at 5:30. Just hav-ing some idea relieves the last-minute "What's for dinner blues"!
* Make friends with your Crock-Pot again. This useful appli-ance can help you feel like someone else is doing all the cooking.
* Every time you start to cook, begin with hot soapy dishwa-ter in your sink and an empty dishwasher. This is why I love to empty mine as soon as it finishes, so it is always empty. This one habit will help your family to help you more.

When they know that only dirty dishes are in the dishwasher, they are more apt to put theirs in there too. Just try it and see how helpful they become. Also, a Post-it note will let them know that they are dirty too.

* Prepare only one item at a time. Get out the necessary ingredients and then put them away when you have gotten them ready to cook. When you are finished, put all the packaging in the trash, veggie scraps in the compost, and refrigerator items in the refrigerator. This way your counter does not get cluttered. It is when we try to do too many things because we are hurried that we get overwhelmed and stuff begins to pile up and close in on us. Clear is easier on our brains.

* Don't cook things on High. Except for boiling water. We SHEs tend to get sidetracked, so it is easy for us to burn a dish and scorch a pot, and this makes more work for us. If you do scorch a pot, liquid dishwasher soap is really good and will loosen up the burnt-on mess overnight. This is the only time you can leave a pot in the sink. LOL.

* As you dirty a dish in preparation, put it in the hot soapy dishwater and either wash it and set it in the drainer or put it in the dishwasher.

* Wear an apron if you have one. This gives you a place to wipe your hands and keep your clothes cleaner.

* Keep a dishrag handy at all times for wiping up spills. Also, if you spill something on the floor, get it up immediately so it will not become a worse dried-on mess. I usually keep my dirty dishrags under the sink so they can dry and I use them to wipe up those spills. Then they get tossed into the washer. I personally do not use many paper towels, but whatever works for you.

* This clean up as you go will make the after-dinner clean up a breeze.
* Delegate to your family setting the table and teach them how. Use your best dishes on occasion and make your meals festive. Put candles on the table and watch your babies' eyes light up.
* I like to serve food onto the plates so I don't have to deal with lots of serving dishes. Do whatever your family likes. Once the plates are filled, I put the pots and pans into my hot soapy dishwater to soak while we are eating dinner. Cleanup is much easier.
* After dinner, have each person be responsible for clearing his or her own plate and silverware. If the dishwasher has been emptied, they will have a place to put them. Keep a small compost bin handy for the scraps. If you don't have a dishwasher, what a great opportunity to enjoy cleaning up the kitchen together and teaching them what needs to be done. Be sure to wipe off the table and counter tops and the splatters on the stove.
* After the dishes are done, wipe down the sink with the dishrag so you will not have water spots, and place it under the sink to dry. Get out some clean ones for tomorrow so your day will start out on the right foot.
* Then all that is left is to sweep the floor. This will only take a few minutes and then you can start the dishwasher and turn out the lights.
* After the dishwasher finishes, I like to put all my dishes away so I don't have to deal with them in the morning. I usually set a timer so I won't forget. Some members set the table for breakfast and set out the cereal boxes.

I know this sounds like too much to do, but after you get the worst part done, keeping the kitchen clean is not very hard, and besides, having a clean, functional kitchen blesses your family with fine meals, interesting conversation, and training for when they have families of their own. What a wonderful legacy to leave them.

You are going to be so surprised at how easy this all is! I promise. Now go shine your sink!

FLYing is Fun when you take it one step at a time.

Do your zone cleaning whether or not you see dirt. One member has taken this on as her motto: **You will never see dirt again!** Are you ready to FLY some more?

Detailed Cleaning List (after you declutter)
ZONE 2: Kitchen

1. Empty refrigerator/clean thoroughly.
2. Clean microwave, inside and out.
3. Clean stove/oven.
4. Wash canisters/knick knacks.
5. Straighten drawers/cupboards.
6. Wipe fingerprints off walls.
7. Wash inside windows.
8. Clean fan/vent, hood filters, and hood.
9. Scrub down cabinet fronts (only a few at a time).
10. Clean light defusing bowls (glass globes over lightbulbs).
11. Clean under sink/throw away old rags.
12. Clean pet dishes.

"As the kitchen goes, so goes the rest of the house."

Zone 3: Main Bathroom, Children's Rooms, and Another Room of Your Choice

Let me ask you some questions about your bathroom:

- If the First Lady of the United States came to your door and needed to use your bathroom, would you tell her it was out of order?
- Do you only clean your bathroom when company is coming and you have two days' notice?
- Do you wait until it is so nasty that you have to wear a respirator/gas mask to walk in there?
- Do you close your eyes when you have to use the bathroom? Or hold your nose and your breath?
- When you finally get around to cleaning this abandoned and most used room in your home, have you asphyxiated yourself with the strong chemical you thought you needed to disinfect the health hazard? I have heard of people who mixed chemicals and died from the noxious fumes they produced. A girl I went to high school with got chemical pneumonia from inhaling this poisonous mixture.
- Can you barely see your reflection in the mirror because of all the toothpaste splatters and dental floss home runs?
- Is there slime mold growing in the bottom of your toothbrush holder or soap dish?
- Have you forgotten what color your sink is, because it is covered with an opaque coating of toothpaste?

And what about your tub and shower?

Oh, you don't want to go there! Well guess what, sisters and brothers, have you ever thought that this could be one hindrance to your getting dressed in the morning?

- Is there mold and mildew covering the walls?
- Does the soap scum cloud up your shower doors and obliterate the gorgeous tile you picked out?

- Does your shower curtain have black streaks from the creases where the water is allowed to turn to mildew?
- Does hair clog your drain and cover the bathroom floor?
- Do you have half-empty bottles of shampoo and conditioner along with full ones?
- Has the bathtub ring taken on a life of its own? Does it seem to be growing?

Now for the other areas of your bathroom:

- Are your counters piled high until you have a hard time finding even the toothpaste?
- Is yucky stuff growing in your toilet?
- Is old makeup taking up your drawer space?

By now you get my drift. So one more question. Aren't you tired of living this way?

Let me explain why your bathroom gets in this kind of shape. It is very simple! You don't have routines. The last time you cleaned your bathroom it took all day and you just don't want to deal with it for a while. You burned yourself out! I have learned a very important secret; a little every day is so much easier than a lot once in a great while!

If you want, try my routine until you have your own established. I swish and swipe every single day. It sounds so easy because it is! It doesn't take expensive cleaners and noxious chemicals to keep a bathroom sparkling! All it takes is your two little hands doing something while you are in there. Yes, you heard me right.

Now, if you need to, you can spend several hours getting it clean TO BEGIN WITH. Keep in mind that I don't want you to obsess about the bathroom;

this is what causes you to burn out and abandon this poor room. Take it 15 minutes at a time or, better yet, each time you go in there do one thing. Clean off the counter, swish the toilet, throw away any empty bottles. If you drink enough water during the day, you will visit this room plenty of times and before you know it, you will have gotten it cleaned.

Did you know that you can clean a bathtub ring while you are in the tub? All it takes is a little bath soap on a washcloth, not cleansers, to get it wiped right off. This is when the "Do it now principle" kicks in. Ten seconds while you are in the tub saves a lot of bending and backache when you try to do this fully dressed.

Supplies:

One of the obstacles that keep us from cleaning our bathrooms daily is not having all the things we need to clean with in the bathroom to start with. I use only two cleaners: a spray bottle of window cleaner and a bottle of all-purpose cleaner. That's it!!! I keep a toilet bowl brush in every bathroom. They cost only a couple of dollars. I also keep it in a holder that I can pour my all-purpose cleaner into. I keep the brush sitting in this disinfecting cleaner all the time. If you have babies or pets around, you will not want to do this. I use a ceramic crock like the one you have holding your kitchen utensils. My brush fits exactly into the opening and all I have to do is pick it up and let it drip, then swish my toilet once a day. I don't have to get out a bottle of cleaner to do this. It is always ready.

You also don't need expensive disinfecting wipes to clean the seat. A little window cleaner on a wad of toilet paper works fine. When you do it every day, it does not get out of hand. As for the hair on the floor, a wad of toilet paper in hand with a spray of window cleaner or just a bit of water will get this up. You don't need a mop;

you will have to bend over or squat to accomplish this. Use your feet if you have to. This is not rocket science: wipe it up!

The same goes for your bathroom sink. It should greet you every morning just like your kitchen sink does: with a smile! Eventually your bathroom will never have to be "spring cleaned" again. I know you don't believe me, but with my daily routines and continual mainte- nance, or shall I say "blessing," I never have to clean like a mad woman because I am too embarrassed for anyone to see how I live.

Here's another way to think about it: Robert and I deserve to be treated like company. Don't you? My bathroom is more than just a place to take care of bodily functions. Now that it is clean and happy, it is where I go to relax, meditate, contemplate, pray, read, and be inspired. I want you to feel this way about your bathroom, too!

Are you ready to FLY some more? Go drink a glass of water! (See you in the bathroom in 30 minutes!) Every time you are in there do some little something! Put up a Post-it note to remind yourself!

DETAILED CLEANING LISTS (after you declutter)
ZONE 3: Bathroom

1. Wash area rugs.
2. Scrub/wax floor.
3. Straighten drawers/cabinets.
4. Clean shower stall/wax.
5. Wash shower door.
6. Clean medicine cabinet.
7. Clean scale.
8. Throw away empty bottles.

ZONE 3: Children's Bedrooms

1. Polish furniture.
2. Straighten drawers/closets.
3. Clean cobwebs.

4. Wash mattress pad/dust rugs.

5. Flip mattresses.

6. Wash curtains.

7. Clean windows.

8. Straighten toy shelves.

9. Clean under the bed.

10. Clean out the closets.

11. Put away stray items.

12. Sort outgrown clothes.

13. Vacuum under beds/closets.

14. Dust baseboards.

15. Clean fingerprints off doors/walls.

16. Rearrange games.

ZONE 3: Extra Bedroom

1. Polish furniture.

2. Straighten drawers/closets.

3. Clean cobwebs.

4. Wash mattress pad/dust rug.

5. Flip mattress.

6. Wash curtains.

7. Wash windows.

8. Clean bay window.

9. Clean bathtub.

10. Clean top of sewing machine.

11. Straighten bookcase.

12. Straighten computer desk.

13. Clean out the closet.

14. Put away stray items.

15. Fertilize plants.

ZONE 3: Children's Bathroom

1. Wash area rugs.

2. Sweep/scrub/wax floor.

3. Straighten drawers/cabinets.
4. Clean shower/tub stall.
5. Wash shower door.
6. Scrub bath toys.
7. Wash down outside of toilet.
8. Throw away empty bottles.

ZONE 3: Office

1. Clear off the surface of your desk.
2. Throw away pens that don't work.
3. Sharpen pencils.
4. Throw out all the trash.
5. Put items to keep in a pending file for Wednesday.
6. Don't stop to pay bills.
7. Straighten one drawer at a time.
8. Toss out receipts older than 7 years.
9. Clean off monitor screen.
10. Fill printer caddy with paper.
11. Establish a place for current bills.
12. Vacuum under your desk and the whole room.
13. Dust all the furniture.
14. Clean any windows.
15. Remove the cobwebs.
16. Check supplies of paper, printer cartridges, stamps, and envelopes.

ZONE 3: Laundry Room

1. Wipe down the top of the washer and dryer.
2. Clean the gunk from under the washer lid.
3. Throw out empty bottles and boxes.
4. Empty the garbage can.
5. Check supplies of laundry detergent, softener, spot remover.
6. Sweep and mop the floor.
7. Remove the cobwebs.
8. Put away all clothes.
9. Look behind appliances for odd socks.

Zone 4: The Master Bedroom

I want you to ask yourself a few questions about this room in your home:

- When you walk past your bedroom do you avert your eyes so you can't see the mess?
- Do you keep the door closed because you don't want anyone else to see your mess?
- Do you have problems getting your children to clean their rooms?
- Does the feel of this room make you smile or cringe?
- Are you tired of tripping over things in the middle of the night?
- Do you sleep here?
- Do you want the room to be restful and inviting?
- Do you want to get up in the night and not bump into things?
- Do you have trouble closing your drawers?
- Can you find the clothes you are looking for?
- Do things fall off the closet shelf and hit you?
- Are you afraid to look under the bed?
- Are clothes piled to the ceiling on the chair in the corner?
- Is your cedar chest filled with stuff you will never wear again?
- Can you walk between the bed and the wall or are there several piles of newspapers, books, trash, and clothes?
- Do you have to crawl into bed from the foot of the bed because there is no room to walk?
- Is stuff piled so high on the dressers and nightstands that you have forgotten what they look like?
- Are the cobwebs becoming moth collectors?

- Are the dust bunnies reproducing in the corners and under the bed?
- Can you see out your bedroom windows?
- Have the spiders decided to winter behind your bed?
- If you open the drapes, does the room fog up from the dust in them?
- Do you know what color your carpet really is?

Now that you have asked yourself these questions, I can hear you saying, "Where do I start?" Remind yourself, as I have said on every page of this book, that this is an on-going process. You may or you may not get the whole room cleaned. That is not our objective.

Before we start, let me share one more story. It begins with a question. Do you have a bedspread you love?

This is why I can't imagine ever sleeping in a messy room again and why this room should be the cleanest room in your home, not your dumping ground for your stash and dash way of cleaning.

It wasn't until I found a quilt that I loved for a bedspread that our room became a sanctuary. At that point I started making my bed every morning. The "made bed" became my SHINY SINK of our bedroom. From there the order started to spread around the room. If you try this, you will see the difference in the atmosphere of your bedroom.

By the way, I also feel that only once your room is clean and peaceful do you have the right to tell your children to clean their rooms. If you don't practice what you preach, you don't have credibility and are not a good example for your babies.

Also, I am not telling you to go out and buy a brand-new bed-spread. For now use what you have. You will still feel the change in your room if you just make your bed and toss some throw pillows on it. If you don't like your bedspread, then you are going to be less inclined to make your bed. Keep searching for a spread that makes you smile. Save all of your spare change. Tell your family you have one picked out at the department store that you would love for a gift. Do you even know what you like? Look in catalogs to find out what your style is. This could be a fun way to window shop.

I found my bedspread on sale. It was a king-sized quilt and it just fit my queen-sized bed as a spread. I only paid $30. It makes me happy every time I walk into our room. In fact, it was the best $30 I ever spent and it took me six months to find it. So start your own bedspread fund if you are not happy with your room. I want you to practice making your bed every morning when you get up and before you leave your room. Just the straightened covers will make your room feel wonderful. Don't tell me that you can't afford to even look at one; I have done a lot of window shopping in my life. If you want something badly enough, you will find a way to save your pennies and get it.

Anything is possible when you set a goal. I want you to FLY and keep in mind that you are worth something and deserve to have a bedroom that makes your heart sing!

Are you ready to Finally Love Your Bedroom?

Any thing you do in this room will be an improvement over the way it was last week. All I am asking is that you do a tiny bit each day — 15 minutes, 30 minutes — I don't care. You can even do the 27 Fling Boogie. Just do something every day over and above your Morning and Before Bed Routines. One time I cleaned a whole room by putting away two items at a time. But I did it every day. If I were industrious I would tackle that job twice a day. Put it in your routines if you have to.

It is time to FLY through Zone 4:

Keep in mind, if you have not decluttered this area, don't even think about doing any of this. Use these detailed cleaning lists to help you get started, after all the clutter is gone.

DETAILED CLEANING LISTS (after you declutter)
ZONE 4: Master Bedroom

"Your bedroom is not a graveyard for stuff that has no home."

1. Polish furniture.

2. Clean off the desks.

3. Clean cobwebs.

4. Wash mattress pad/dust ruffle.

5. Flip mattress.

6. Empty trash.

7. Wash windows

8. Cull some books from bookcase.

9. Straighten drawers.

10. Clean under the bed.

ZONE 4: Closet
1. Straighten the top shelves.
2. Arrange the shoes.
3. Take suitcases to basement.
4. Dust shoe bookcase.

ZONE 4: Master Bathroom

1. Wash area rugs.
2. Scrub/wax floor.
3. Straighten drawers/cabinet.
4. Clean shower stall/wax.
5. Wash shower door.
6. Clean medicine cabinet.
7. Clean scale.
8. Throw away empty bottles.

YOUR BEDROOM IS NOT A GRAVEYARD FOR STUFF THAT HAS NO HOME! If you don't stop this, it is going to be your grave.

This is the room that is the heart of your family and your marriage. It should give you joy when you walk in there and fill your heart with peace. It is where your babies were conceived and you love your husband. If you are single, it is where you snuggle in for the evening with a good book to fall asleep. This is the room that you wake up in and go to sleep in. It is imperative that this room be the cleanest in the house. From this moment on, you are not allowed to pile stuff in this room. Do not fold clothes in this room. (We all know what happens there. We fold them, but never put them away.)

I have counseled many women about this room. I have found over the months that when this room gets clean the rest of the house falls right into place. It becomes a haven from the chaos in the home, your hiding place. I have also found that when this room is clean, with no clutter piled up, that most women rest better and have more energy.

I also feel that when we are sick, this room can promote healing or keep us sick. When all that clutter is everywhere, it is so hard to feel peace. Clutter lays guilt on our heads. We beat ourselves up about it, and we make ourselves sick with the stress it puts on our system. Get rid of the clutter and you will see the veil of stress lift and, I believe, sickness will leave your body. Guilt is a terrible shadow to live under.

So many women have never felt peace. This is my main wish for you, to find the peace I have. I don't want to hear that you have this disease or that, and that your clutter didn't cause your illness. Stress is the main cause for illness in our country and the world. If we relieve the stress we will all be better off. We are not our diseases. We can learn to live with and find peace in any situation.

It is a mind-set. "What you think about, you bring about." I learned this from motivational speaker Rita Davenport many years ago. If you think you are a picture of health, even if you may be sick, chances are you will feel better. There is no sense feeling sorry for ourselves. Learn to live with what you have, and don't let it get you down. I have a dear friend who has many problems, but she has learned to adapt and she calls herself handicapable. She always sees the glass half full.

I have a challenge for you. If you have a desk in your bedroom, I want you to find a new home for it. We know what our desks look like, stuff piled to the ceiling, stuff that needs to be done and is calling to us. I am not telling you to do this right this instant. I want you to think about this for a while and come up with a plan.

FLYing is so easy when you have a peaceful bedroom!

Zone 5: The Living Room

Zone 5 is our living room/family room/den. If you have two of these areas or even all three, I only want you to do one this month. After a few months, you will have them decluttered and detailed cleaning will be a breeze. I promise it will only get easier. We are going to continue to declutter this zone.

Detailed Cleaning List (after you declutter)
ZONE 5: Living Room/Family Room/Den

1. Clean cobwebs
2. Clean windows
3. Straighten bookcases
4. Wash ornaments and what-nots
5. Clean out end tables
6. Straighten closets/drawers

7. Wipe fingerprints from walls

8. Polish furniture

9. Clean out magazine racks

10. Clean phone

11. Clean under cushions

12. Clean out fireplace

13. Move furniture and vacuum

14. Shampoo carpet

If you have a family room, game room, sun porch or other room that is used by the family for living purposes, then concentrate on decluttering one room each month or as you find more time. Do not push yourself. They did not get cluttered in one month and they will not get clean in one week. Remember, Babysteps! If you are unable to do any task, just skip it and go to the next one.

Another question:

What is your living room? Have you ever asked yourself this question?

- Is it a dumping ground?
- Is it a formal room for guests only?
- Is it a room that has lost its appeal?
- Is it a comfort zone that is loved by all?
- Have you ever really established what you want your living room to be?

Let me tell you what your living room should NOT be: a room full of Hot Spots, a laundry folding center, an after-school dumping ground, a playroom with toys permanently attached to the floor, or a long-term crafting area.

Some of you may have formal living rooms and then have family rooms as well. But to us they are both living rooms, even if you call your main living area where your family congregates a family room, the living room zone applies to this room. If you have both types of rooms, they both get addressed during this zone. Don't get overwhelmed. Spend 15 minutes in each room, each day. Be consistent.

As you have heard, shortly after the FlyLady community began in December 1999, God sent me a wonderful person named Kelly. She e-mailed me offering to help, but I didn't know if anyone else could be as bossy as I am or could understand the solutions I'd found. I began to ask her questions and give her tests. I talked to her husband and found out that their home was in good order, not perfect, and that she had gone from total CHAOS to peace in about a year's time. My husband thought I was answering my own e-mails. Kelly sounded just like me. Since her initiation, she has been my right hand. Here is her personal story about "zones":

"I have a little confession about my living room. My dear sweet children kept walking in the door from school each day and just dropping all of their things into the living room. I realized that this was making me crazy and I had to establish a place for backpacks and shoes. I found a pretty laundry basket that my Mom had given me and I placed it near the front door where it looked nice and still out of the way. This is where the backpacks and shoes were to go each day. My son did very well with the change but my daughter did not. She would still come in and drop her stuff in the living room. I warned her that if it didn't stop, I would throw her backpack out the front door.

"Well, that day came. She dumped her stuff and walked into the kitchen. I stood there looking at the backpack, picked it up, and tossed it out the front door onto the lawn. A while later she went

in search of her backpack and couldn't find it. I told her that she would have to look for it where I told her it would be. She thought long and hard and finally opened the front door and there it was. She was in shock that I actually did it! She still occasionally back-slides, but I will give her a warning shout that I am about to toss it and she will come running. It has become a joke, but she knows that there is a place for her things.

"Establishing a place for the things that are constantly dumped in the living room will help change the family's attitude about that room being a dumping zone. It begins with you. You have to get rid of your Hot Spots in that room first. You can't expect your family to not dump anything when you have not set the example.

"Work hard this week to declutter your Hot Spots in the living room. Try to establish a home for things. This might not get completed this week, but you will be on your way."

Several months ago I got a message from one of our members.
She began:

"Could you please help me? I am at a roadblock. Because of the past I am used to only cleaning when I see something slimy, moldy, or fuzzy growing. I have since cleaned everything and my home looks pretty good. The problem is that when I do my zones, I'm not cleaning these areas because they aren't 'dirty enough' yet. It feels weird to sweep the floors when there is only a little dirt or wash the shower walls because I don't see anything needing to be washed off.

"I guess I need a lecture on preventative medicine or some-thing. Thank you, in advance, for straightening my thinking out. I

know that just writing this is helping me see my distorted view of things."

My answer to her:

It will only take minutes for you to do the zone stuff. A few minutes here will save you major time when the slime starts growing. You will never see dirt again.

This is the perfectionist in you. We love to see the dirt we have cleaned up.

The next message from her:

" 'You will never see dirt again.' You wrote that after I shared that I don't feel right cleaning unless something is 'dirty enough.'

"I have been saying this over and over in my head since I read it. That is now my motto! I now want to be excited when I go to clean my zone and there is no dirt. Then I will clean the area anyway to keep it that way.

"What a lightbulb moment!

"Thank you! :o)"

Dear FlyLady...

THE BENEFITS OF FLYING—ROMANCE AND MUCH MORE

Got your attention, didn't I, Marla? Well, it wasn't just a cheap line to get your attention, it's the truth. FlyLady got me sex. And lots of it!

My husband and I are soon to celebrate our ninth wedding anniversary. Like many couples that have been together for a while, we slipped into sort of a rut. A comfortable rut, but a rut where there wasn't a lot of romance or hanky panky. Okay, there wasn't ANY. There was the once a month or so "obligation sex." Wheee. There had to be more to life, but I didn't know what it was. I just figured we were getting older and that was the way marriages were once you went past 30.

After three babies, I had gained weight and didn't much care. I was just a housewife, who was gonna see me, right? And why bother to put makeup on, right? Steve and Blue and Oprah don't care if I have pretty hair, right? And housework? Yuck! No one appreciated me, so why should I — it just got messy again anyway, right? (Gee, does that sounds like Franny or what?????)

When hubby came home to a dirty, messy, cluttered house and a chubby wife wearing slobby clothes and not even caring if her hair was combed. Gee, I am just so surprised that he wasn't happier to be here and wanting to whisk me off my feet to the bedroom. (Note the heavy sarcasm.) It took a brick wall named FlyLady to whack me in the head to figure that out...

Well, in August, my friend told me about FlyLady. I was

skeptical. I went to your website. I read the shoe thing and right away knew that you were insane. No one wears shoes all day. I hate shoes. I was almost ready to click that corner and obliterate your happy little face from my screen when I saw the one thing that changed everything.

The picture of FRANNY. That was ME! That sad, pathetic looking thing with icky hair and fuzzy slippers. THAT WAS ME!!!!!!!!!!!!!!!! I wanted to look like the pretty, smiling FlyLady. But how????? Well, I clicked around your site and kept reading. Printed a few things out. I still thought you were insane because of the shoe thing, but I figured I had nothing to lose, so I said I'd start the day the kids started school.

So, I cleaned my sink. Mmmm, that wasn't nearly as tough as I thought it would be, and it really DID make my kitchen look nicer. I left and ran some errands. I came home, and my door to outside is in my kitchen, so my kitchen is the first thing I see when I come home. Mmmmm. That looked SO nice when I walked in. Later that afternoon I set my timer and did one counter top at a time. I felt like a real dork setting a timer for 15 minutes. The way I grew up, if you didn't spend 7 hours on Saturday cleaning, you weren't cleaning. What the heck could I accomplish in 15 minutes??? Now that I know better and know how much I can do in 15 minutes, I am thinking of having a timer surgically attached to my arm — man, I just LOVE the timer system! I wanted to walk in my house and have that feeling I had when I saw that sink — but I wanted the whole kitchen in on the deal. Little by little, my whole kitchen became a wonderful retreat. It looked good and was such a beautiful sight to come home to!!!! Oh, I had to spread this to the rest of the house!!!!!!!!

Then that shoe thing. I hated that at first. I really, really hated it. But, it's funny. I have grown to hate not having my shoes on. I can go let the dogs out whenever they need to, not wait until they are barking and crossing their legs and whining. I can take the garbage out NOW because I have shoes on, and my garbage is never too full. I can do SO many more things ... and I have the softest, sexiest feet now — my skanky old calluses are GONE! A little lotion in the socks every morning does wonders — and it's only been 2 months!

Now, you ask, how did I get a bunch of sex out of a clean sink and shoes? Bear with me, I am getting there. LOL! Little by little, FlyLady invaded my home and my heart. I started caring about what I looked like. I started wearing makeup. I started cleaning. I started decluttering. Oooh, that was so much FUN. Throwing all that old crap away was SO liberating. I was taking back my house from the CHAOS monster. And I found out our house wasn't nearly as yucky as it seemed. It's actually quite nice!

Well, all this caring about what I looked like and running around to the Goodwill and running out to let the dogs out and all, I somehow lost 15 pounds. And, add that to looking prettier and having nice skin now from my morning skin routine, well, hubby was starting to notice. He also noticed the cleaner home. Oh man, that was a huge turn on for him. LOL! Instead of coming home to a yucky home, he came home to a peaceful retreat where his wife cared enough about him to make things beautiful, and because it was beautiful, I was happier — and men REALLY notice that. Well, as my house got cleaner, I couldn't stand that I still smoked and was reeking up my nice house, so I quit. It's been over a month now. Oh my God, thank you for that. You've helped make my life longer!

So, you add up a wife that cares about her home and makes it nice. A wife that is busy and has more self confidence because at the end of the day she feels that she accomplished something. A wife that looks sexy because she didn't sit on her franny all day. A wife with beautiful skin because she took 2 minutes in the morning to wash her face and put on moisturizer. A wife with sexy soft feet. A wife that is peaceful and doesn't holler at everyone anymore because she just feels so good about herself! A wife that quit smoking and spent her cigarette money on lingerie. (tee hee hee)

Now, take that and add it to a husband that LOVES having a nice, peaceful, organized home. A husband that sees the changes in his wife's attitude and notices there's less of her tush to notice — ha ha. A husband that is rather old fashioned and sees his wife keeping the house clean as a sign that she loves and respects him. (You women libbers keep your nose out of that comment — we are old fashioned and we like it. LOL) And a husband that LOVES walking in at the end of the day and seeing the supper table set, his newspaper in his spot, and something nummy bubbling in the Crock-Pot instead of saying "What's for supper?" and seeing a wife with a blank look in her eyes who starts calling Pizza Hut.

Now, take a wife like that, and a husband like that and what do you get? A HUBBY WHO CAN'T KEEP HIS HANDS OFF HIS WIFE! *giggling madly* He's like a teenager!!!!!!!! I asked him what was going on and he said "The Fly thingie." I said, "HUH?" He said, "Honey, the house looks great, YOU look great, and you seem so happy, and darn, you smell good today, and … Well, I can't tell you what else he said. *more giggling*

So, in one website, you've given me the knowledge,

strength and wisdom to make my house beautiful, make me more self confident and beautiful, make myself healthier by losing weight and quitting smoking, and renewed some serious sparks in my marriage. WOW!

Now, my kids figure into the sex thing, too. Before you go turning me in to Child Protection Services, hear me out! We have a 3-, 7- and 8-year-old. A 3-, 7- and 8-year-old that can never seem to get settled into bed. A crabby mom that's yelling until 11pm to quit talking, settle down and go to sleep! ARGH! Not conducive to hanky panky. Well, when I set up my daily routines, I set up ones for them, too. Instead of me suddenly looking at the clock and going, "Argh, it's 10pm, and you have school tomorrow, get in bed now," we have a wonderful routine. It includes baths at a set time, and a half an hour of mommy reading each night — if they even make it until I am done reading before they zonk out, it's a miracle.

Now that their rooms have been decluttered, they've stopped waking up in the night and having bad dreams and they all sleep through the night. I agree with them, too. I sleep MUCH better in my pretty bedroom, too. It only makes sense that they would as well. Now, instead of crabby evenings, the kids are in bed at a reasonable hour, they sleep in their beds all night, and me and Daddy have a couple hours in the evening just for us. We relax. We talk like real people, we laugh, we watch grown up TV. And then we go to bed. It's wonderful. He's become my best friend all over again!

Thank you from my heart ...

Jenny from Minnesota

FlyLady's watching you

You've heard from me several times. I ended up backsliding and was so totally embarrassed. I found out it was because my DH was home for 6 months, and he really messed up my routine! Now he's back on the road and my routine has kicked right back in. Anyway, the reason I'm writing is so I can tell you about my 5-year-old daughter. She just loves the FlyLady Clingies [stickers of the FlyLady cartoon]. She is constantly moving them so I never know where I will find you next.

She says "FlyLady helps you clean and you have to keep every room clean," so you do have an eye on me! Well, my daughter needed something for show and tell; they aren't to take toys, they are to take something special to them. Previous items have been family pictures, a coin her daddy gave her and so on. So she takes you to school with her. The teacher told me what she said when she did her show and tell. First, she stuck you on the wall and told the kids and teacher that FlyLady will help them keep the classroom clean, then when it was her turn she said, "FlyLady is special because she helps my mom clean the house and keep it clean, so now anyone can come over whenever they want. Mommy also has cookies for you, because she has a clean kitchen; she can cook more." Well I had to tell the teacher just who you were and explain. She said it sounds like her house (she's a single mom of a 6-month-old and a teacher to 23 kindergardeners!) with no internet access, but I'm printing routines out for her.
FlyBaby D.

START YOUR DAY OFF GLOWING

In a whispered voice, I asked: "Hey, honey, what is that?"

Sleepily he replied, "Hunnhh?"

I shook him and said, "There's a glow coming from the kitchen. Go see what it is."

"Don't you remember? That's just your clean sink!"

"Oh, yeah!" I mused, contentedly.

I smiled as I fell asleep again, knowing that in the morning I would be greeted by my clean and glowing sink.

I am a FlyBaby who resisted starting with the sink. I cleaned up other areas and started making my bed every morning, but all I could hear was "Is your sink shining?" So one day I spent a good hour cleaning and shining it. The next morning my husband said he wasn't really awake until he walked in the kitchen and the shiny sink woke him up! I find myself cleaning it a few times a day so I won't ever have to spend an hour cleaning it again.

I look forward to implementing more of your routines in my life. Thank you for caring so much about us SHEs!

Pam from Nevada

FlyLady Is for Everyone: Including YOU!

If you are tired of living in CHAOS, this can help you if you are a man or woman, old or young, retired, working full time, or home all day long. This will help *anyone* with a home.

What are "Payroll SHEs"?

These days many people work either outside the home, in the home, or part time. They are "Payroll SHEs." Because of their circumstances, they are not sure that FlyLady is for them. But they are wrong. This system works for Payroll SHEs as well as for "SAHMs" (Stay At Home Moms).

I want you to utilize some of the tips we are going to share with you. So many SAHMs say, "Oh I have all day to do this." Do not allow yourself to get caught up in this inefficient way of thinking. The more time you take, the longer it will take to do something.

Payroll SHEs, for the most part, know how important every minute of every day can be. If you have been struggling with the "not enough hours in the day" syndrome, then listen up. This message is just for you.

I have heard every excuse in the world. Even though I don't allow whining, many of you continue to tell me that this system can't possibly work if you have to leave home for your job. I am so sick and tired of hearing this. My Granny always said, "Can't never could do anything!" So if you are not willing to try some of our tips and continue to complain, then you may not be ready for our way of thinking. If you are willing, then keep reading. Let me begin by saying that I wish all my members pretended to be Payroll SHEs. This would help them make good use of every minute they have.

You have chosen to go to work; it is a fact of life. Many of us do it, and, yes, I consider myself a Payroll SHE. Now, don't fuss that I don't understand. You have no idea of my schedule with my County Commission job and the hours that I put in working on FlyLady. For many years I worked outside the home and I know exactly what it is like to have to leave the house and come home to cook, as well as keep up with the laundry and household chores and raise a family. Whether you have made this choice out of necessity or it is a career decision, it doesn't matter. You are working outside your home. Whatever the reason, there is a certain attitude adjustment that comes with this decision.

How many times have you thought, "I work all day, why do I have to do all of this? Why can't I just be waited on?" I know you are frustrated, but we can help you to stop this whiny thinking and get on with your life. That is a martyred lifestyle. Since you feel so bad that you have to work, you make everyone around you miserable. Only you can change this attitude to one of "Oh well, I work and my job blesses my family!" Be thankful you have a job and can provide for their financial needs. But I am going to tell you how to provide for your physical and spiritual needs and your family's.

Part of your frustration comes from the stress of the house being a mess and your perfectionist attitude. Yes, perfectionism rears its ugly head once again. We were brainwashed by Madison Avenue to believe that we could have it all: the happy family, the wonderful career, and a fulfilling lifestyle. I am here to tell you that it is possible, but the attitude that I am too good to clean a toilet is not part of this peaceful solution.

We have many members that are Payroll SHEs. I know that you are successful whether working outside the home, inside, part-time, home-schooling, or anything else — we feel that what you do during the day is a job.

So, here are some things to keep in mind:
- This system does work for you!
- How to make this work so you don't have to clean on the weekends, and can enjoy family time!
- You can take time for yourself.
- You can cook even with a busy schedule.
- You will be able to plan ahead for your week.
- How you can jumpstart your day!
- The price your family pays because you are a martyr.

I know that you have spent several years feeling overworked and frazzled. Most of the time, after a tiring day of running around like your head was cut off, you can see absolutely nothing that you have accomplished. I know just how tired you feel. Your day has been spent running around putting out one fire and then the next. Oh, and we are so good at dealing with crisis situations. In fact, we pride ourselves on being really good under pressure.

We have all seen the juggler that can keep several plates spinning on several poles at one time. Do you feel like this person most of the time? Running every which way, being forced to jump to keep the plates from hitting the ground. What happens if you stop? You think you would have a lot of broken plates. I have a little secret. We don't let the plates fall off the poles. We grab them in full spin and set them on the counter!

I know your frustration. Running around putting out fires is not very productive work. Guess why? You are letting the problems set your schedule for the day. Kelly and I are giving you the tools to address these spinning plates once and for all time. The stress level you have put yourself under is not good for your health or your family.

Each time you are in the midst of spinning those plates, think about why you are forced to juggle them.

1. You didn't pay a bill on time so you are running around trying to get it paid before the electric company turns off your power, or the phone company shuts down your service. You have the money in the bank, but you just forgot to pay the bill. Not having the money is another problem and, believe it or not, this system will help you with that, too.

2. It is 6:00 PM and you have no clue what's for supper. Your children are hungry, so you pile everyone in the car and go for fast food. The guilt levels are rising and money is being spent on food that is not that good for your body. No wonder you can't lose weight or there is no money to pay the bills.

3. Getting yourself and the family dressed is a pain because you don't have clean clothes. They are sitting in the dryer and were not quite dry when the dryer stopped and they have soured. Or they are wadded up in the laundry basket and not fit to wear because of all the wrinkles. Or, even worse, they are in piles all over the house and have never been washed to start with. You know that sick feeling when your child needs her baseball uniform and it is at the bottom of the laundry pile because it just slipped your mind. There were just too many loads to do, so you became overwhelmed and did nothing. Guess what? Out of sight, out of mind does not work for this problem.

4. You need to leave the house for an appointment and you can't find your car keys. Don't you just hate that helpless feeling? And the more you search, the later you become and the more stressed you feel. That doesn't even begin to address the fact that you were running late to begin with because you were having a hard time finding something to wear.

Do you see the vicious cycle of spinning plates? One is just about to hit the floor!

Do you want out of this frantic juggling circus act?

Here are the steps. If you have been listening to us you are already starting by establishing small routines for your morning and evening. Oh, and put on your lace-up shoes!

As part of your routines, we ask you to think about your day, think about tomorrow, and think about next week. This simple act, called "planning," is going to help you quit spinning your plates. No longer will you be stomping out fires or trying to keep the plates from hitting the floor; you will be in control of your schedule. As you stop the plates from spinning you will find more time for the important things in life. The daily maintenance of your home and yourself becomes automatic.

This will not happen overnight. So we teach you to establish one habit at a time. As each new habit becomes part of your routine, you are taking that plate off the pole and putting it in the cupboard.

Eventually you will be in total control, and only have one plate to spin on rare occasions. You will find that peace is contagious. The more you implement your routines, the easier it is to add new habits.

This is called behavior modification. You are going to have to wean yourself off the adrenaline rush that you have been getting from the CHAOS. So the next time you feel yourself spinning plates, take 5 minutes and look at what caused this circus act. I'll bet it can be traced to something you refused to do or didn't even think about until it was too late.

Are you ready to FLY without spinning plates?

I realize that you are tired when you come home from work and it doesn't get any easier when this FlyLady person gives you home-work assignments. A peaceful existence doesn't happen overnight. It is a process of adjusting your negative thinking and building on your routines. Life is too short to wallow in self-pity because you have to work. It is time to get over it and deal with what is! The reality is, you have a home. Everyone that works — men and women, single or mar-ried, leave work to return to their home. And yes, they all have toilets that can get pretty nasty if someone doesn't swish them occasionally.

Your attitude has to change from "Why do I have to do this?!" to "This is my home and I deserve to have a wonderful place to live. This blesses my home and my family and, most of all, me!" Do you feel the difference that these two statements make in your heart? Giving up this martyred attitude and taking on the persona of doing good for yourself and your family relieves you of stress! If you understand this small reality and embrace it, I have done my job.

You also have another attitude that is going to be the death of you: "I have no time for myself!" So after everyone has gone to bed you stay up later and later, until you are barely getting enough sleep to function the next day. Then, in the morning, you hit the snooze button four or five times and by the time you finally drag yourself out of bed, you are already running late. This makes for a stressed out, nasty attitude, yelling at your babies and running around like your head is cut off, not knowing where to turn or what to do next. The solution is so simple! GO TO BED AT A DECENT HOUR!

Getting your rest will stop this downward spiral! With enough sleep you will be able to get up and spend some quiet time getting ready before you have to get the children up and dressed. Just fifteen minutes before the rest of the family will make a world of difference in your stress level. When you get up and get dressed before the rest of the family, you can accomplish those other tasks that keep your home maintained and running smoothly. You know, the tasks on your Morning Routine that seem so impossible to accomplish because you haven't got the time. This is the perfectionist again. Say it the way it really is, because you don't think you have got the time. Most of what we teach is to think ahead. Just a few minutes the night before thinking about the next day will relieve most of the stress.

"Go to bed at a decent hour!"

Let me walk you through an evening. The key to a calm morning is a Before Bed Routine. This goes for all of you. Even if your home is still trashed, you can do this!

1. Lay out your clothes for the next day. If you have children, teach them to do the same thing or do it for the babies.

2. Put everything you are going to need tomorrow beside your launch pad (the front door).

3. Check your schedule to see where everyone in the family is going to be for supper and get an idea of the weather so you can pick out the proper clothes and umbrella, if needed.

4. Locate your purse and keys and put them by the door, too. There is nothing worse than being late because you can't find your keys.

5. Everyone is going to be home for supper, so what do you have to fix? Take something out of the freezer and put it in the refrigerator. Don't forget the side dishes. I am not telling you to fix them, just think about it. It is a sad picture when you have a chicken thawed and nothing to go with it. A little planning now is so much easier than waiting till the last minute and beating yourself up because you have forgotten something once again.

6. Make a to-do list or grocery list if you need to pick up a few items before you come home or on your lunch hour. Try your best to not stop by the grocery on your way home; it wastes valuable time. Just start a list.

7. Get everyone that can to shower before bed. That way, the next morning you may only need to wash hair or just wet it and style it. This saves me lots of time, although I love bubble baths before bed to relax me so I sleep better.

8. Go to bed with your kitchen clean or as straight as possible and your sink shining.

9. Then get into bed and go to sleep at a decent hour. You are going to be so surprised at the difference this will make tomorrow.

Now that you have gotten enough rest, when the alarm goes off you can get up and dress without the hassle of being stressed. Make sure you set the alarm so you get up before the flow of the family.

This will become your sacred time for yourself. You have had your days and nights mixed up for a long time; it may take a few weeks to regulate your internal clock. You know how cranky babies get when their days and nights are mixed up. This has to start with you!

If you really want to break this vicious cycle, you will start this tonight. I have always said that the Before Bed Routine was the most important to this system. If you do nothing else, you will begin to feel the Peace that I have been telling you about for months.

So you don't get dressed first in the morning.

There is no excuse for skipping this step — I have heard them all and I have an answer for every one:

• **I might get my clothes dirty before I leave for work.**

Have you ever heard of a duster or an apron? It is not like you are going to get down on your hands and knees and scrub the floor before you leave for work! My Granny would always get dressed to shoes and then put on her lightweight cotton housecoat over her clothes in order to work around the house. I prefer an old favorite denim jumper. Many others like to put on a smock or an apron.

• **The baby has to nurse before I leave.**

I understand that this can be a problem, but there are ways to make it easier. Get as dressed as possible, including fixing your hair and face. This also means hose (if you have to wear it)! Put on a robe. Then, after the baby is nursed, you can just throw on your good clothes. This will only take a minute because you have laid them out the night before.

Another way to do this is to feed the sweet babe snuggled in your jammies before you get up. Then get both of you dressed after the feeding/snuggle time. What a wonderful way to start your day.

• **I can't fix breakfast in my good clothes.**

This is the same ole excuse. Wear an apron, duster, or smock over your clothes.

- **I can't do any bathroom cleaning in my good clothes.**

You are done while you are standing in there naked or in your PJs. All you do is wipe down the counters, put the toothpaste and makeup away, and swish the toilet. Now was that so hard?

- **I like to sit and enjoy my coffee and newspaper when I first get up.**

So I guess you are afraid that you are going to spill coffee on yourself or get newsprint on your clothes and hands. Here we go again with the same answer: put on an apron, smock, or how about a bib? Don't you usually eat and drink at work, too? How do you get around making a mess on your clothes? Napkins!

- **I have to get our lunches ready.**

Most of this can be done the night before as you are cleaning up from supper; one less job in the morning. Just remember to give your husband's lunch to him or tell him where it is kept in the refrigerator.

- **I wear heels at work; you can't possibly expect me to run around the house in them.**

No, I don't expect you to wear heels around the house. I want you to wear shoes that make you feel energized. If you have done your Before Bed Routine, your dress shoes will be laid out. It is a good idea to put them by your launch pad the night before so you won't run off to work in your sneakers. Or, just in case, keep a pair of old black pumps in the trunk of your car!

- **I don't have time; my babies wake up and need me!**

Then you are not going to bed at a decent hour and you're dragging your Franny out of bed 15 seconds before your babies wake up. It is very important to start your day off ahead of the commotion that comes when the rest of the family gets up. I feel that it is similar to putting on your oxygen mask first on an airplane when there is an emergency. You can't help anyone else if you don't do this.

• **I can't get dressed in 15 minutes; you are crazy!**

I know you have not been able to do this in the past because you were too busy searching for your clothes, getting the children dressed, and doing the ironing-board shuffle. You know exactly what I am talking about. This is when you try to iron something while you are still wearing it. There is also the problem that the blouse you want is still wet and has to be dried. When you take care of your clothes the night before you eliminate these stressful minutes from your life and add peaceful moments in their place. Once your children are doing this, too, your whole day changes.

• **I like to wait until just before I walk out the door!**

That is because you are usually dressing in the car on the way to work. Are you one of those ladies that puts on mascara while you are driving? I want this to stop. The stress that you feel because you are trying frantically to get dressed and look decent for your job will go away if you will just do what I have asked. Your morning will become a time of joy and peace. Your attitude will change from the grouchy mother to the sweet, gentle-voiced, loving mom. I wish this peace on you, but it is not going to happen unless you try this one step.

This works whether you are in college full time, working shifts, home-schooling, working at home, or staying at home! It is essential that we all get up and get moving first thing when we wake up! This means dressed to shoes, with your hair and face fixed, too. I don't care who you are or what you do for a living.

Are you ready to FLY through your morning stress-free?

What About Being Late?

Now that I have walked you through your Before Bed Routine and part of your Morning Routine, we are going to look at actually getting your Franny out the door and to work on time for a change.

Many of you are habitually late! This is a common trait among our members. Our husbands hate it, too. Believe it or not, this has to do with our martyred attitude. Tardiness is a passive-aggressive behavior. I know you don't think it is! We are in control when we make people wait for us, consciously or unconsciously! The problem also arises because of our perfectionism; I just need to do one other thing! This may become more of a problem after you have your routines in place. I find myself wanting to answer one more e-mail or the phone as I am walking out the door. I have learned to stop that behavior.

So what is making us late? We are the reason. It is because of our lack of thinking ahead. When we put a little forethought to our day and take precautions to keep ourselves from getting off track, we are on time. This is why our Before Bed Routine is so important for a peaceful start to our day.

Ask yourself:

How much time do you spend searching for things? If you could put your hands on an item when you need it, it could save you precious time every day. Right now, where are your car keys? I keep mine clipped to my purse. Before I get out of the car, I hook them to my purse. I never have to hunt for my keys. That used to be a big problem for me.

I would get down to the car and then have to run back up to the house to search for my keys. I have also hidden a key in my car in a magnetic case, just in case my SHEness comes up again. Last year, I had a terrible incident where I got locked out of my car by accident during a thunderstorm. I learned a hard lesson. I had to break a little window to get in and unlock the car. It was a very dangerous situation because of the lightning and I was way out in the middle of the forest with a teenage fishing buddy and his uncle. I was responsible for that child, and his safety was more important than a broken window at the time. If you have ever had to break a window, you know it is not easy. Now I keep a key hidden and check on it once a month so I will never be left standing in a lightning storm with a fly rod in my hand again.

Do you search for bills that need to be paid? When I first found Pam and Peggy in the 1980s, I devised a notebook similar to the Control Journal, except I didn't have routines in it. This was a portable, zippered notebook with a handle. It had pockets, zippered pouches and it could hold a three-ring binder. I'll bet you have one laying around the house right this minute. In this notebook I kept my bills to be paid, my check stubs, my file for my paid bills (at that time I kept every receipt; I don't do that anymore), pens, pencils, notebook paper, my menus, grocery list, greeting cards, thank-you notes, paper clips, little stapler, and stamps. This became my portable office. At work, on my break, I could work on my menus or grocery list or, at lunch, I could pay a few bills and work on my budget. This was a quiet time during which I could take 15-20 minutes of uninterrupted time and take care of our finances, plan our menus, and make out a grocery list. My notebook was always with me. In our Basic Weekly Plan, when you balance your checkbook, simply spend an hour at your desk; you don't have to do it all at once. Take little snippets of time and over a week accomplish some of these guilt-laden tasks that are continually put off until they are a raging fire and need immediate attention. Putting this off only makes it worse.

Another reason we run late is we don't fill our cars up with gas when it is convenient. We wait till we are smack dab on empty and we are running behind schedule. This costs us time and safety.

Running late makes us rush and rushing can cause us to be careless. Keep a $20 bill hidden for emergencies or that opportune time to fill up. I also keep a $100 dollar bill stashed for larger problems. I rarely have to use it, but I know I have it, if needed. This gives me a sense of relief and that translates into less stress in my life. I have even done this when I only had thirteen cents to my name. It took a while to save it up, but I did it. I learned this lesson from Rita Davenport's *Time Management* tapes from the 1980's. (They are no longer in print, but her book is in most libraries: *Making Time, Making Money.*) I still keep motivational tapes in my car! My car is a rolling university. Why not spend commute time in behavior modification and inspiration sessions?

We have to curb our thinking! When we hear ourselves say, "I can do that later!" let this be the trigger that tells you, "Right away is the easy way!" Putting things off usually makes them more difficult to do. The reality is we think, we dread, and we continue to procrastinate until it just has to be done. The whole time we are beating ourselves up over not doing the task when it was so simple. My Sweet Darling calls this the "Do It Now Principle." You know that awful feeling when you should have put that roll of toilet paper in the holder when you first thought about it, and now you really, really need it!!! When you think about something that could be so simple to do right now, don't put it off until later. I am talking about very short, simple jobs that will save time and energy if done now. You know what everyone's Granny always said, "A stitch in time, saves nine!"

Learning to act in advance, instead of reacting later, will help you add precious minutes to your day. Eventually this will become a habit and you will surprise yourself. I have had to look in my checkbook and make sure I had paid a bill because I did it without even thinking. That is a wonderful feeling!

Dear FlyLady...

I CAN **FLY** TOO

I am a Payroll SHE who began subscribing to your service a few months ago. I work part-time and tend to two young children ages 5 and 2. My work takes me away from home at times and when it doesn't, I work from home. As such, I have a full-time babysitter/housekeeper.

I'm married twenty-one years now. I spent the first sixteen years of my marriage collecting college degrees and working full time on my career. Though my husband and I have lived in our present home since 1983, I can honestly say that I have never made this house a home, or, more accurately, I haven't ever made any strides toward making my house a home until benefiting from your services. I never had the time nor the inclination to do so.

After my children were born, however, I not only wanted to make a home for my family but I wanted to save my sanity from the lack of organization in this long-neglected warehouse. We'd been collecting "stuff" for so many years and just putting it away in closets without any rhyme or reason. Before my recent cleaning efforts, some areas of my house were literally untouched since we moved in 18 years ago.

Though I was always organized in my career and at my place of business, I was a mess at home. To make matters worse, my babysitter/housekeeper is, and always has been, an excellent babysitter and a terrible housekeeper. She doesn't put anything away in the same place twice. I used to spend hours of my days looking for things.

And in her defense, there has always been too much clutter

in this house and no real designated places to put anything. There wasn't any leadership nor any organization. My husband was always badgering me about my disorganization and it was frustrating to both of us. I felt defensive and depressed about it quite often.

I had heard about FlyLady from a parenting loop I was involved in. After subscribing to your kind service, I simply read my mail and the reminders without daring to try. That's always been my problem with the house. I never knew how to begin. It seemed so overwhelming and futile to even start.

After a few weeks I started with shining my sink. I was very resistant to wearing shoes in the morning because I just never have. I've always prided myself in being the freestyle individual who doesn't wear shoes as much as possible and NEVER gets in routines, or ruts, as I would call them.

I must admit that I loved the look of the clean sink and, quite naturally following, the surrounding areas when they were clean. Yes, the cleanliness spread from the sink to the counters to the kitchen table and, yes, one day I got dressed to my shoes. I've been faithful to my morning and evening routines since. Routines are no longer a dirty word to me. They are my sanity savers.

I have done quite a bit of decluttering in the last couple of months, but still have a way to go. With consistency, so far I've cleared about half of the clutter in this house. No mere trifling feat. I've recently started the monthly zone work and have worked all this month on my dungeon, making a sizeable dent in my dumping ground, a.k.a. the garage.

My house looks clean on any day and I know where things are most of the time. I've relieved my babysitter of most of her housekeeping duties and soon will be looking for a part-time babysitter only. My husband never wanted to make do with a part-time babysitter though I've only worked part time because he thought the house would be a total shambles if someone else wasn't working on it. He never thought I'd keep up the house, and told me so.

But now my husband is very proud of me, and says so on most days. My children, young as they are, have followed my lead without my even saying a word to them about pitching in to help out. My five-year-old loves to help me clean, especially if we set a timer. My friends have commented on how wonderful my house looks and how much more energy I seem to have. I love being connected to my home and the way that connection has wrapped my entire family in this push, this clear, cathartic swell of enthusiasm and spiritual uplifting.

Thank you for your help.

Pam from California

FLYING WITH HEALTH ISSUES

I just had to write.

I am a single mom of 3 girls under 9, and have just returned to full-time work after 5 years spent at home coming to terms with clinical depression.

When your site was passed to me by a friend, I will admit I was skeptical, but I had a look, and now I'll never look back.

I have struggled for years trying to cope and not fail, subsequently perfectionism has taken its toll on my health and the health of my family. NOT ANYMORE!!

My house is semi-sparkling (I am still learning to FLY), I have time for my children and time for the new man in my life, but most of all I have time for myself, which is the one thing that always suffered as a result of my often fruitless labors.

I have adapted the plan to suit me and mine. I actually follow the plan a week in arrears, so the first week I started to fly I started generally decluttering and building a strategy. While doing this each evening I picked up my Zone Mail and planned it in for the following week. I am unable to put aside an hour to do my Home Blessing Hour, so I divided it up throughout the week in 15-minute bursts — Wow! What a difference that made. Like many others I have found my children following suit and putting dishes straight into the washer instead of leaving them for the Cleaning Fairy!

I have just read a mail item about the children that encouraged me to write this note. My daughter (9) has been so impressed with this system that we have developed her own plan, lovingly called FlyKids, which has finally put pay to the major disaster area known as her bedroom. Using the exact same strategies we have developed easy routines which take care of homework, gymnastics training, clubs, play, and bedroom cleaning. I never thought I would see the floor in that room.

Once again, a great idea which has finally brought peace and harmony into our world of CHAOS!!!
'Setta from Plymouth, United Kingdom

FLYing—IT HARDLY SEEMS LIKE WORK
THANK YOU THANK YOU THANK YOU!!!

Your site and instructions are the greatest! I have got to be the world's worst when it comes to clutter, but not anymore! My 10-year-old son says that I am scaring him with all this organization. Oh well, he's even getting into it a bit. At least he leaves my shiny sink alone and puts his dishes in the dishwasher! I guess you could call me a FlyInfant cuz I've only been at this for a week.

I'm also a Payroll FlyInfant, but I'm starting to get the routine down in the morning before school and work. My co-workers just shake their heads in amazement of what I can get done before work and on my lunch hour. Thank you again, at least I can now let folks come into my kitchen/dining room and my entrance. Can't wait to put out a major fire in my post-holiday living room (though my decorations are down and put away).
Thank you again,
Julie from California

I have been on your list for about three weeks and I appreciate all the work that you do. I have a husband of 19 months (and loving every minute of it) and am working full-time. The day before I heard about your e-mail group, I was beginning to think that I needed a new way of keeping our town house in order. I am home only two evenings a week (one of those I do grocery shopping) and only home one day on the weekend. I wasn't ever able to keep our little house tidy or clean. I am very thankful to your discipline and tips in housework.

I am establishing my routines at the moment. I only made our bed when I changed our sheets, our bathroom used to only be cleaned every two or three weeks (you can imagine how dirty the tub was), and I would wake up most mornings stressed because I didn't have my clothes organized and I would end up falling asleep trying to decide what to wear, which meant I got up later than supposed to, then I would have to find my clothes and iron them. The first morning after I subscribed to your group I started making our bed, it is so nice to be at work knowing that our bedroom is tidy. Then I started tidying our bathroom daily and spraying our shower with one of those sprays that eliminate scrubbing (when I arrive home in the evenings, the bathroom looks so good), and now I am trying to organize both mine and my husband's clothes the night before. This morning, I didn't wake up cranky and stressed.

I am not able to implement the reminders or the zones (as I am not home very much), but I do take notes from them. I really appreciate you dedicating this week to Payroll SHE's. Each day I look forward to what tips you have in there for me. Thank you for writing to us Payroll SHE's.

One day I will be a SAHM and look forward to it very much, but until then I have to learn how to maintain our nest in the world while I am working outside the home.

Thanks again for all that you do.

A FlyBabe from Australia

You can start over anytime

I just want to say thank you. You have been a Godsend. I am a mother of a 2 year old, and I teach 5th grade. I started "flying" last winter after I saw a blurb about you on our local news (KSN — Anita Cochran) and never really got the hang of it, until this summer. I decided this summer that I was going to do the whole thing, so I just jumped in with both feet. It worked wonderfully! I started back to school on August 13 and was so busy there that I didn't "fly" that week. It drove me nuts to walk in the house.

Finally, last week I asked my DH (a no-clutter kind of guy) to pick up our little girl from the sitter's so that I could come home & start cleaning. When they got home, they chipped in. Within an hour, we had our house back to some sort of normalcy. It was great! We did our weekly cleaning again tonight, and I am feeling good about the house again. Tonight as I was putting the dust mop away, my husband gave me a kiss on the forehead and told me what a good housekeeper I was! He never would have said that a year ago! He went on to say that FlyLady had helped around here.

I also want to say that those who feel like they will never make this a habit need to give it a while. I can't stand to have my kitchen not picked up and clean now. I make sure every night that the sink is clean, and it really helps to get fresh towels out for every day.

Thanks again!!

Amy from Kansas

Getting the Whole Family to FLY

When you picked up this book, I know you were searching for a way to get your home in order. I have heard you all say it many times: "If only I could get some help around here. My husband (wife) is the messy one and my children tear things up faster than I can clean it up, so why even bother?"

Let's look at our homes with a focus on encouraging our children to help. In order to get their full participation it has to be fun and there needs to be a reward afterwards.

Let's look at our Weekly Home Blessing Hour.

We have seven items on our list to do:

1. Empty trash (all over the house)

2. Dust

3. Vacuum

4. Mop

5. Cull old magazines

6. Change sheets

7. Polish mirrors and doors

Now, how can we get the family involved? By making a game of it. Save the jobs that are the hardest for you. If you are going to be picky about the way they do it, then don't play this game; it won't be fun for anyone.

KEEP THIS RULE IN MIND:

HOUSEWORK DONE INCORRECTLY STILL BLESSES YOUR FAMILY!

Have fun!

Decide on a good reward for getting the home blessing done without complaints, fussing, or fighting.

- Going to the park
- Swimming
- Ice cream cones
- Snow cone or slushes
- Taking in a matinee or renting a movie and popping popcorn

You know what your children love to do.

"Children love routines. They know what to expect and when. They also know what is expected of them."

List the items on a small sheet of paper. Then put them in a bag or a bowl and have them draw their assignment. Do not hold the children to your standards; this is supposed to be fun, not perfect. Do you understand this? Set a timer for 10 minutes and go have some fun. After the buzzer goes off draw another assignment. Afterwards, go have fun. You can hold your older children to a little higher standards, but not perfection. I don't even hold you to that tough goal. BabySteps! The more they do this, the better they will get at it.

Another way is to get the children to work with you: for instance, if you are dusting, give them the feather duster and teach them how to use it without knocking things over. Take a dust cloth and together you can dust the furniture top to bottom. Remember, children are short and can get the lower spots easily.

Have them help you vacuum. Put a basket in the middle of the room and have them put everything in it before you run the vacuum cleaner. You could even have them aim for the basket, if you allow tossing in the house. Then let them push the vacuum around the room. Remember, only the middles, we are not doing under the couches just yet.

Now for mopping. You sweep the kitchen floor while the children get on their bathing suits. This is from one of our members: Put some wet towels on the floor with a little more water, and let them scoot around on the floor on their Frannies. Have a spray bottle filled with plain water to add to the excitement. You could also put a tiny bit of baby shampoo on the floor for soap. Remember, it doesn't have to be perfect, just fun. You get the floor clean and they get to be silly. They will love it. You can let them play as long as they are having fun. Then toss the dirty towels and swimsuits in the washer.

You can do the bathroom this way, too, then put the children in the tub and let them play. But they have to be cleaning in there, too. It isn't the type of cleaner that gets things clean, it is the act of doing the cleaning that accomplishes the task. We don't have a magic potion. A little shampoo on a washcloth will remove a bathtub ring. As for culling magazines, you can turn this into a learning event. Have them look for a magazine with last month's date on it.

Changing sheets is not that hard. One of my fondest memories is when my father taught me to make hospital corners. Every time I put clean sheets on our bed I think about him. You can set a timer for this, too, and race to see who gets them in the laundry room first. Each bed needs two sets of sheets, so you don't have to wait for the laundry to put the fresh sheets on the bed.

Polishing mirrors and doors doesn't have to be perfect either. Just a little spray of your favorite cleaner on a paper towel or cloth and let them get the worst of it off. You will be surprised at how good the doors will look without dog nose prints and hand prints on them.

As for gathering up all the trash in the house, teach them that emptying the trash means putting a new bag in the trash can. Keep extra bags in the bottom of each can so they don't have to go searching for them. Blow your whistle. Have them run to their rooms and gather up trash. You can also put on their favorite music. You can stand anything for an hour! Let them know this is the way you get in the mood to clean; you have to set the stage for fun. This goes for you, too.

So do you see what I am doing here? Creating a fun time for blessing your home with the children helping. You can do this! Ask the children for suggestions and have fun.

Home Blessing with FLYing Children Power!
Making it fun gets the job done!

"Sprinkle your words of love, encouragement, and teaching all over your home."

Dear FlyLady...

YOU KNOW YOU'VE BEEN FLYWASHED WHEN ...

Dear FlyLady,

You can tell you've been FLYwashed when someone gives you a home-decor catalog and you prefer the Before picture (with only a chair, table, table runner, and a few books) over the After picture (piled with the STUFF they want you to buy).

You can tell you've been FLYwashed when your neighbor calls and starts complaining about the mess she's living in and you tell her, "NO WHINING ALLOWED," to set the timer for 15 minutes and to get off her Franny and go shine the sink!

You can tell you've been FLYwashed when you break your toe and are unable to wear your lace-up shoe and you miss your shoe!

You can tell you've been FLYwashed when you get out of bed and make the bed — in a hotel!

You can tell you've been FLYwashed when your (born-organized) mother comes over and decides to clean under the fridge and you smile as all she finds is a little dust, then she decides to clean off the top of the fridge and all she finds is — you got it — a little dust. (See BO mom look perplexed!)

You can tell you've been FLYwashed when your husband walks into a peaceful house and says, "I need to thank this FlyLady for a happy wife!"

Keep up the good work! Sprouting flight feathers,

Wendy from Idaho!

ROUTINES WILL GET YOU THROUGH ...

Dear FlyLady,

Today I buried my beloved dog, Gunner, whom we have had for 7 years. Putting him down has crushed me. I didn't think I could face today, knowing what I had to do ... but thanks to the Flying lessons, I was able to rise, wash my face, get dressed to my shoes, and face the day.

Did I look good? No. My eyes were swollen and red, my face pale, and my clothes dirty from the digging. Did I survive? Yes. Thanks to FlyLady, I have hit my Hot Spots, Blessed my House (I needed to keep myself busy, so I did it ahead one day), I know where my laundry is, set out my clothes for tomorrow, and have indulged in a long, hot bubble bath.

I'm taking BabySteps until this pain subsides a bit. Each bit of cleaning reminds me of something our beloved Gunner did. Sweeping up his hair in the kitchen, mopping his paw prints for the last time, and even cleaning out the refrigerator and spotting the last can of Alpo.

At least he had a good life. Until I learned to declutter, I did yell at him more than I should have, but after months of Flying clutter-free, I learned to enjoy his puppy-ish ways. Our family, now peaceful from my Flying was able to love him and pamper him in the manner he deserved. What would have been a "suicidal-thought day" a year ago, was a "survivable day" today, and I believe it was because I had focus. I had e-mails to remind me that life must go on, that I only had to do BabySteps, that it was ok if I wasn't "Perfect Mom/Born-Organized Mom" today — all taught to me by YOU, FlyLady.

Thanks for helping me survive today. I look forward to BabySteps and e-mail to help me survive tomorrow. I don't mind all the e-mail ... please, keep it coming! Even the Subject

Line helps remind me to put one foot in front of the other (once I have put on my shoes) and live.
Julie from Illinois

Dear FlyLady,

Let's play "follow the leader!"

Do kids notice? You bet they do! I have a 5 1/2-year-old, a 3 1/2-year-old, an 18-month-old, and 4-month-old. The 5 1/2-year-old saw me picking out my clothes the other day and asked what I was doing. I told him I pick my clothes out the night before to make it easier in the morning. After he went to bed tonight, I noticed that he had picked out his clothes for morning! :) This was made much easier by the fact that we just went through his & his brothers' closet. We matched up pants & shirts, and hung them on a hanger together. We got rid of things they didn't love (no more itchy sweaters!) and now they can dress themselves in the morning and they look terrific!

My daughter is 18 months and is just learning how to talk. Every morning she says, SHOES! SHOES! SHOES! until I put on her shoes :) Does that make her the littlest FlyBaby? Also I made a morning & evening list for the kids and covered it with contact paper and put it on the fridge. They love being able to check things off every day, and I love not nagging. I just tell them, "Check your list!"

Thanks FlyLady!
Lois from New Hampshire

MY STRENGTH IS IN MY SHOES

Hello FlyLady,

It is not like me to write feedback, but I feel compelled after this last week. I have been learning to fly now for about 5 months and every time I got discouraged, you stuck with me. I didn't realize what a life-altering system this was until I attended a Labor Review class last week. My baby is due in 3 weeks, my sister was a gem and went with me to the class since my DH had to work.

At one point, the instructor went around the room and asked each mommy-to-be to name one thing that would empower her — something that makes her feel strong! I didn't even have to think about it — I was first to answer and mine was, "my shoes!" My sister looked at me with a confused stare. I think she was somewhat embarrassed because the other ladies went on to say things like "my husband," or "a picture of my kids."

I explained to my sister that all of those things made me strong but for some reason I felt like I could conquer anything as long as I had my shoes on. Well, I — of course — know where the whole "shoe" thing came from, but it has been my little secret. You see, my extended family was all pretty much BO and they would laugh if they knew — but I find comfort and acceptance in your system. I have shared my great find with a certain SHE friend whom I knew would respect it; but other than that, no one knows.

My sister told my husband, parents, and everyone at my baby shower — one lady seemed to understand. She said "If we handled everything in life like a sporting event (with our shoes on and our minds focused) we would probably find strength we didn't know we had."

Thanks for helping me to find my strength. I am prepared for this baby. We are having a house built and I can't wait to treat it like a castle — now that I know how!

Thanks again! Flying in California

Now you are anxious to find out how to get your husband (wife) to help around the house! After all, it is their home too; why should you do all the work? I have heard it thousands of times. We have to start with your attitude in order to get some group participation here.

From the beginning of our little cyber-family, I have always insisted on our main rule: No Whining Allowed!! We have all caught ourselves in a whining mode. When was the last time you let whiny words ooze out of your mouth? This morning?!!

Why do people feel the need to whine? Let's explore this for a bit.

Frustration: The house is getting on your nerves! People seem to be piling on your workload. You don't feel like you are accomplishing anything. So you just have to let out this frustration so the world knows that you are being mistreated. Think about this for a minute. This is a cry for help, but you don't know how to ask for it. You are feeling sorry for yourself too. You want someone to listen, but that is not happening because, let's face it, no one hears a whiner. This is also a martyr attitude rearing its ugly head.

Depression: The pressure of the house, your schedule, and the things left undone slowly digging your grave. The whine is another cry for help — even if it is unproductive. You have never been taught any other way to seek help. I want to help you change this fruitless behavior. When you realize that this has no effect on your family except to tune you out, then you can initiate productive behaviors. It all goes back to being a martyr.

Attention-Seeking Behavior: We have all done this: Our cries for help fall on barren ears, because we have cried wolf too many times. Just like the little shepherd boy: His cries were ignored because he had been seeking attention. It is only when we give ourselves the attention we need and are not searching for outside attention that our requests for help will be answered. I know you don't believe me, but changing this one character trait in yourself will change your life and actually get the help you desire.

Why do you think I want you to FLY?!

Self-Pity: This one is probably the most destructive, because you act pitiful and unloved. If the truth were known, you are unloved, but it is not by your family — it is by yourself. You are not taking care of your own needs first. If you don't love yourself first, you are unable to love others to the fullest extent of your being. This is not being selfish. Who is going to take care of you if you don't!

We have all heard Rodney Dangerfield's famous line: "I get no respect!" The reason he gets no respect is that he does not respect himself. Demand it of yourself and you will not allow disrespect from others. This does not happen overnight. As Dangerfield whines to his audience, it may seem funny to us at the time, but in real life, our families just turn down the volume. Our whining becomes background noise! Would you like to see their ears perk up?!! I can teach you how to get their attention, and it is so easy!!

STOP YOUR WHINING COLD TURKEY!

This is easy. Now that you can see and hear your effects on your family, you can stop yourself from doing this. Now, here is the fun part. You can blow them right out of the water by setting an example and doing what needs to be done with a cheerful attitude and out of love for your family. Even if you are not feeling very cheerful at the time, bite your lip and put a smile on your lovely face, just for the fun of it. The results will reinforce this happy attitude and you will start to feel the inner change in yourself.

When you start FLYing, housework no longer is a chore, something to be dreaded. It becomes a way to bless your family, yourself, and your home. I want you to have the peace that I have. This came from my change in attitude toward everyday tasks.

Do not whine to me that it is not fair that you have to do it all, that your family should help you because they live here too and your husband doesn't lift a finger to assist you. I don't want to hear it. If you want your family to help, you can get their support without even asking by setting the example in love, and before you know it you will have the help you want.

Husbands (Wives):
You must be waiting to find out if I have a magic potion that will get your husband (wife) to help around the house. I don't, but you do and it all starts with you. Now, don't whine.

Your home has been messy for a very long time and just because you have read this book isn't going to make things change overnight. After all, your husband has seen you read lots of other books on getting organized, and look where they have gotten you. If you look closely, he is just as frustrated about all the clutter too, but he doesn't have a clue as to where to start either. So he just says nothing. Don't get caught in the trap of wanting him to notice changes in your home. Let me warn you. He will be afraid to say a word for fear that he will jinx whatever is going on.

You are the one who picked up this book. I can't change anyone in your home but you, and I am not going to teach you how to manipulate your husband. You hold the answer and it starts with your attitude toward your home, your family, and yourself.

When you can, set the example in love and show your family that you do care. Then you will start to see a change in them. This attitude adjustment starts with you, and before long the family will be helping. I know you don't believe me.

Here is what will work:
1. Stop whining.
2. Do your routines consistently.
3. Stop keeping score.
4. Just do what needs to be done. Don't stand around with your arms crossed waiting for someone else to do it. If the undone job is affecting your ability to get your routines accomplished, then just do it! Don't nag! Or expect them to read your mind. There will be time for delegating later. First you have to do it for *you*!
5. Quit seeking approval for doing a job. We have all said it: "You didn't even notice that I cleaned up the bathroom."
6. You can't change anyone but you. It is your example that is going to set the tone for your home. When it is done with a loving attitude, they will take notice and start to help.

Right now all I care about is how your attitude is affecting you. If you allow stress, anger, and self-pity to build up, you are not taking care of yourself. Please do this for you. When you accomplish this, you will be blessing yourself and your home.

Dear FlyLady...

MY HUSBAND IS HELPING

I've been on this list for just over a month. I didn't even tell DH about it, 'cause I knew he'd say that it was just another project I was starting that I wouldn't finish. I began by doing Morning & Before Bed Routines. I have slowly added weekly routines and zones.

This past Monday, DH's work schedule changed from 8–5 to 10–7. I had been making the bed in the mornings before we left for work, but with him leaving later than me, I didn't have the opportunity. Every evening this week, I have come home to a bed that is mostly made. He apparently refuses to put the frou-frou pillows on, but everything else is done. The laundry also makes it into the hamper, or at least onto the floor next to the hamper, but that's far better than spread around the bathroom and bedroom.

DH did all this without my even asking. No nagging, nothing. Absolutely amazing. This is totally unlike him. In 5 years of living together, he has NEVER made the bed, and rarely picks up his dirty clothes off the floor.

Result? I'm in a great mood when he gets home, and so he's in a great mood too. We have had more time this week to eat dinner together (in our kitchen that's always clean now!) and do projects around the house.

I love this list and I will be sticking with it. I guess it's finally time to tell DH the reason behind my change!
FLY Baby Shannon from Oklahoma City

FlyLady's Definition of Marriage:

I started my mentoring group to help women get their lives in order. It was not to teach them how to badger their husbands to help in the home.

Many have complained that I don't understand that husbands and wives have an equal responsibility in keeping the home working. YES, I do know this. But unless your husband or wife is a part of this group, I can't help them. I can only help you. I don't expect you to do it all, but you can and thousands have. What about the single moms or widows that have to do it all by themselves? Does no one care about them? They don't have husbands to help. They have to take care of the whole home alone. Oh, and I almost forgot the members whose spouses are in the military and away from home for months at a time; also the spouses who have to travel a lot for their jobs. They have the responsibility for the entire home on their shoulders.

What I have noticed is that when the member of our group, either the husband or the wife, gets their routines in place and the clutter in the home is decreased, they have found that the other spouse comes around and starts to help, and so do the children. They start to clean up their "off limits" HOT SPOTS! You know, the ones that if you even touch will get you in HOT WATER!

Marriage is not a 50-50 proposition, as many of you think. I believe that this perception is hurting many families. Here is why.

When we feel we are doing our half of the work, we automatically feel slighted because we don't feel our mate is doing his or her fair share. So we pout, fuss, or even go on strike. This is silly.

Marriage is a 100% proposition for both people. Each person giving their all to the family. When you do all you can, you have done your best. When you sit at the computer all day, don't get dressed, and don't hit a "lick at a snake," you are not spending your time wisely. All because your perception is "Why should I clean up, it is just going to get messed up again!" or "He won't even help, this isn't all my job! If he won't help, then it can just stay this way; I didn't make the mess, so why should I clean it!"

There are many reasons for our members to not get their Frannies up and moving. Most are just excuses. We all have the same number of hours in each day. Even members with several children are seeing progress. There are members with sickness who are doing well and there are members who work either at home or away from home who are seeing great progress.

So what is your excuse? Are you sitting pouting 'cause your spouse does not do his or her fair share? You can only change yourself and your own attitude. Get the mote out of your eye first. As you set the example, by getting your HOT SPOTS clean, you are going to be so surprised at the changes in your family.

12
Do You Know Where Your Laundry Is?

Laundry is a never-ending cycle: sort, wash, dry, fold, and put away.

It is like a child that does not get the proper attention. You can catch it hanging out in unsavory places: mildewed in hampers; stinky and soured in washers for days; cold and wrinkled in dryers; wadded up in baskets stashed beside beds; or folded nice and neat and left abandoned in the laundry room.

If you will give your laundry the attention it needs, it will not grow up to become an unruly pile that consumes your home, time, and peace of mind.

You Can Conquer The Laundry.
There are several approaches.

Think about laundry as a 5-step process: sort, wash, dry, fold or hang, and put away. When you leave out any of the ingredients, the laundry takes on a life of its own and one that is not so pretty.

Maybe we need to think of laundry as a baby that can't be left unattended or a pot of food cooking on the stove. We have to keep it in the back of our minds all the time. I even have to set a timer or I forget that I have put a load in the washer. What if we made a rule? No! Rules don't work for us. It has to be a routine.

My washer and dryer are in the basement. Sometimes when I need to work in the basement, I have found that if I spend the 35 minutes in the basement while the washer is running I can kill two birds with one stone — keep my mind on the project at hand and clean off a shelf or sort through some stuff to give away in that dungeon we pretend is a basement.

We are so easily sidetracked when it comes to laundry. How often you do laundry depends on the size of your family. In a perfect world I would do a load on Mondays, Wednesdays, and Fridays. True confession here. I am not the best at keeping up with this and Robert helps me quite a bit. He actually enjoys doing it.

"Kelly says 'Your dryer is not a laundry basket.'"

Have I ever told you just how blessed I am? The hard part is getting it started, following through to the dry, and then folding and putting it away.

Oh, sorry, that is all of it, isn't it? So we have worked out a deal. He puts the load in the washer and then the dryer, and hangs up the good clothes as they come out of the dryer. Then he brings up the basket of clean unfolded laundry and sets it in front of my face (per my request). He puts it on the footstool that I keep my laptop on. Talk about the "Do It Now" principle!

This has been working well. I get up and go fold and put away the clothes while they are still warm from the dryer. Teamwork. (He does not have a talent for putting them in the drawers. He would live out of the laundry basket.) His excuse is, "I don't know where your clothes go." I used to not know this either. I had to put Post-it notes on the drawers for a long time. I am getting better. So I can put them away and purge something at the same time.

If your drawers are too full and you are unable to put your clothes in them, spend 5 minutes tossing some of the stuff that is unworn. Give it away! It will make your life much easier.

So now you have heard my true confession about my problems with laundry.

Some of you are not laying out your clothes in the evening. Instead, you are dragging around in the morning looking for something to wear and putting off getting dressed until the last minute. I want you to stop this.

The best way to get a handle on this behavior is to plan ahead. I know these are bad words for sidetracked people, but this is what will remedy your "sidetrackedness." One of our members suggested this: as you are doing the laundry, put together your outfits. Do this for your children, too. Put their whole outfit on a hanger or in a folded-up group. Hang it on a hook in the closet separate from the rest of the clothes or in a drawer that is just for their outfits.

I know this is a change from the way you have always folded your clothes in neat little stacks of socks, underwear, and T-shirts. This way makes more sense. We take it off as an outfit, why not put it away as a complete ensemble almost all the way to shoes? This is great for children and adults.

With children you are not trying to find the socks that go with that outfit. With adults, you can be packed at a moment's notice for a trip. Try it. I know it is hard to do things differently, but new can be fun and it just might help alleviate your getting-dressed problem.

As we have agreed above, all of us have to do laundry, some only a couple of loads a week, while others have a dozen. It affects us all the same way, we put it off until it gets to be such a big job that we are paralyzed by the thought of it. You know exactly what I am talking about: **piles of dirty laundry on your bedroom floor that just keep growing.**

Do you want to know why they continue to multiply? Perhaps the reason is that you have too many clothes because you have compensated for not doing laundry by buying more clothes to cover this problem. Then you struggle for two days to finish it all, but it never really gets put away because your drawers are too full to put anything away. So then you live out of a clothes basket or the piles on top of the dresser or dumped on your bed or in a chair. After a while you can't tell the dirty ones from the clean ones, so they all get tossed back into the dirty clothes pile.

How in the world can I stop you from doing this to yourself?

Let me tell you how I quit doing this to myself: I cleaned out one drawer for myself and one for each family member. Then I labeled the drawers so I would know where to put the clothes.

At one time, when I lived alone, I would let everything I owned get dirty before I would go to the laundry and do them. (I did not have a washer or dryer.) I mean two huge garbage bags of dirty clothes. Did I tell you I had too many clothes? Then I would go to the laundromat and spend half a day getting them done. At least they were done, but I would start the vicious, draining cycle all over again. I could go several weeks without doing the laundry.

My remedy was to cut out some of the steps that would trip me up and keep me from taking the first step to doing the laundry. Sorting!! As I took off my dirty clothes, I would sort them into a dark basket and a light basket. Yes, I actually have a dark-colored and a light-colored basket to remind me to sort. Robert does it, too. In fact, I think he taught me this. He also taught me to take my socks off, right side out. Push them down over your heels and then pull the toes. Poof, your socks are right side out. No more having to turn socks after they are washed. I love this part.

So now as a basket gets almost full, I can do a small load and it actually takes less time than a huge one. It is no longer over-whelming to me. It gets put away much faster, too. And the socks are easier to match. I hated that part, but not anymore.

Now, you have to have a simple routine to accomplish this. I have it included in my morning routine. As I leave my bedroom in the morning, I grab one of the baskets that looks almost full and take it to the basement. Turn on the washer, then come upstairs and set my timer for 40 minutes. This is how long it takes for my washer to do a load. Do not leave the washer running while you are going away from home. Just stop the washer and let them soak. Do not leave appliances running when no one is home. Also, have a smoke alarm in the area of the washer and dryer. Many home fires are started here.

After the washer has stopped, grab some hangers and head for the dryer. Put the clothes in the dryer. Now when the buzzer goes off, you will already have the hangers at the dryer. Here is the rule! You have to go to the dryer when you hear the first buzzer. No excuses. Hang up the good clothes first, put the rest in the basket, and take them to the room where they belong. I have a secret, I do not fold underwear. I just put it in the drawer. Then I mate the socks and fold everything else in the small basket. I have timed myself and I can do this in 2 minutes. I'll wager you can, too.

I don't have to do a load every day, but I check my baskets to see if I do, every single day. It is so much easier to do when you just have a routine for it. This is why I have three reminders every

169

day to keep you on top of your laundry. It is so easy to forget. This reminder is one of our most beloved.

KID Note: When my son, Justin, was 9 years old, he started to do his own laundry. Did you know that children tend to mess up fewer clothes when they are doing their own laundry? Even 6-year-olds can be taught to do laundry with a little help. Get them their own color-coded baskets for their closets.

"Nothing says 'I love you' like clean underwear!"

Dear FlyLady...

LAUNDRY NEEDS ROUTINES, TOO

So, I've finally got it … hit right between the eyes. It's about the laundry … the whole do the load thru — wash, dry, fold & put-away thing. I thought that I could keep up with the laundry by doing all the laundry every other day … but I was still leaving the last two loads either in process or in baskets. Then one day I was super busy on laundry day and I remembered that FlyLady says not to put in a load unless you finish it all the way thru … So, I did only one load that day. Completely. Then the next day I tried it again. This time I did two loads — all the way thru. I was so happy … I didn't have to fold any laundry the next day or find a forgotten load in the dryer! I was free to start it again. It's been a week now and I'm completely caught up with the laundry. I have just put in a load of my older boys' stuff and I have to go change it over. Then once it is dried, I'm folding it and putting it away myself! It'll take me only minutes to do it.

Thanks so much for this list.

Katrina from Pennsylvania

LAUNDRY IS A FAMILY AFFAIR

Dear FlyLady,

You are right, children can do their own laundry. Each of my children has his own laundry basket in his room, and has a laundry day assigned to him. They are not allowed to do their laundry any other day, so if they don't take the time to do it on their day, they have to wait till the next week. They have been sorting and doing their own laundry since they were five. The only help they needed after having it explained to them, with a few reminders, was a footstool at the machines so they could reach. None of their friends can believe that they do their own laundry, and hardly any of my friends can believe that I haven't done my kids' wash for years.

Why is it that mothers think they have to do everything for their kids? My kids know how to do almost everything in the house and can take care of themselves, if they need to. There won't be any panic when they go away to college, and I'm not creating sons who are totally dependent on their wives for everything. My mother-in-law taught all of her eight sons to cook and I am eternally grateful! Thanks again for all your encouragement.

Ann-Marie from New Hampshire

13

Paper Clutter: You Don't Have to Save Everything!

Let's talk about our paper clutter!!

You all have it, so let's see exactly what it amounts to.

Let's look at each area of clutter one at a time!

1. Piles of newspapers

Did you know that by the time you get around to reading a day-old newspaper you would have heard most of it on the radio or TV?

Instead of holding on to them so you can read when you get a chance, discard them every day when the next paper comes. If you go two or three days without reading, save yourself some money and discontinue those newspapers. You will be rid of the clutter and the guilt from not reading what you have paid good money for. Try reading online or listening to the National Public Radio stations. You will be surprised at how much news you pick up without even having to concentrate. I never read a newspaper except to see if I have been quoted correctly as a County Commissioner. Robert tells me to check and see what "Cilley Says."

Now for those coupons that come in the newspapers. If you haven't used them, then why buy the paper? For SHEs, coupons are a challenge. But once you get organized, you will use your Wednesday desk day to clip and save while you make out your grocery list. For now, set them aside or give them to someone you know that will use them. The guilt you feel when you see these unused coupons or go to the grocery without them is not worth a dime. I want you happy, not guilt ridden.

2. Baskets of unread magazines

This is a biggie for every SHE I know and love. We hate to part with our beloved magazines. We might actually need something we have seen or we might miss a good article. Baloney!! If you have seen something in a magazine, just go and try to find it again. You can see it in your mind's eye, but there is no way you are ever going to find the magazine you saw it in. Without a reader's guide, you are hopelessly lost. So why waste hours searching for a picture when you can go online and find your answer if you really need it? If you receive magazines in the mail that you never open and read, then rethink the money you are spending each year on the subscription. If you have a basket of magazines that you hate to part with, it is easier if you do it on a weekly basis. This is why I purge magazines each week. I put them in my car and as I go about my week, I drop them off in different places that I go to: meetings, doctors' offices, car service centers, the courthouse, offices. Just think about having to wait in a waiting room with five-year-old magazines. How about getting your car worked on and there are only men's magazines? That is why I take the opportunity to get them out of my home and put them where they will be appreciated.

Also, if I have not read them, I take the time to do so before I leave them in the waiting rooms.

One other thing I do: I have an Exacto knife by my chair and a notebook with lots of sheet protectors. If I see an article that I want to keep or a picture for my "want" book, I cut it out right then and there. It is my magazine; no one will miss it. I have my book of "likes and keeps" without having to spend hours searching for a certain magazine. Now that our kitchen is almost finished, I can throw away my kitchen want book. I have completed that dream. No need to hold on to it. I have a garden book, too.

3. Junk mail

Throw it away as soon as it comes to the house. It does not even deserve the right to enter your home. Throw it away, shred it, or burn it. Be careful with those credit card applications we get daily in the mail. Tear out the name and numbers. I throw them in my fireplace.

"I know that every flat surface in your home has a pile of paper on it … made of junk mail!"

4. Boxes of old school papers (from college, or kids' papers)

Do you still have a box full of papers from high school or college? Get rid of that stuff. It was another life. You are not going to need the books or the papers with those grades. We had rather not remember.

Now for your children's papers: These are hard to part with, but let your children decide. If your children are grown, give them back to them. Or save only a special one from each year for their scrapbook. Not every paper is a keepsake, believe it or not. If you save everything, that diminishes the value of those special ones. They get lost in the clutter.

5. Recipes

We SHEs are addicted to cookbooks and recipes. But how often do we use them? We dream of being this wonderful cook, but the truth is we cook the same ole things all the time. What happens when you want to find a recipe you saw in some magazine or cookbook in your library or drawer of recipes? You can't find it! I have reduced the number of cookbooks that I have. I've kept only the ones I love. Also, my Sweet Darling is a wonderful cookie baker. He has his very own cookbooks. I had to be very careful when I decluttered our cookbooks. I accidentally took his favorite cookie cookbook with adjustments from years of testing to the truck to be given away. I was lucky; I had not taken them to the Humane Society Thrift Shop. So, as you clear that clutter, make sure it is yours to give away.

6. Paperback books

If you have read them, pass them on to someone else or give them to the library or a hospital.

7. Piles of unopened mail

If you have not opened it in three months, then it is probably trash anyway. Open the newest mail first and toss the old bills. Sometimes you can just look at the date and toss. It is important to look carefully since it may be something like a credit card that could be found by someone. Sort the old mail over a trash can.

8. Tax papers

Do you have tax papers from 20 years ago? If so, there is no need to keep them. Our tax papers fit in one manila envelope. Our copies of the tax returns, receipts, and directions for the schedules are all in this envelope. This takes no room at all. We also have a file for receipts that affect the cost basis of our home.

This is all that we keep. We do have 20 years' worth, but they only take up five inches in a file drawer. Each envelope is labeled. We don't keep every cancelled check but we keep our check registers. Our check registers tell our history if needed. Make sure you check with your accountant, attorney, or financial advisor about which papers to retain and for how long.

9. Medical records

Children's shots records are needed until they start college, and sometimes up until the girls become wives and mothers to prove that they have had a rubella shot. Health departments have been known to purge records without contacting you. That happened to me and I had to have another shot. Not fun; I don't like them.

10. Paid bill receipts

We only keep insurance receipts and tax deductible cancelled checks. For all of the others I have a check to prove that I have paid them. All other receipts go in the trash and get burned in the fireplace.

11. Old phone books

Get rid of them. I keep one old one in my car for when I need a phone number or address.

12. Catalogs

We all have these. We love to look at them. They keep coming every day. Get rid of them. If you want to order something, then do it and toss the catalog. Don't hold on to these. Besides, there are many online catalogs.

13. **Bank statements**

We balance them and toss them, keeping only the checks we need for tax purposes and our house cost basis. The rest are burned.

14. **File cabinets — full of who knows what!**

We need to go through these files and toss. There is hardly anything that we really need to file. I have two crates that I started two years ago when I became a County Commissioner. I have not looked in those files for a year and a half. This tells me that I didn't need to waste my time filing the stuff. So now I read my memos and file in the trash can. The trash can is my favorite filing cabinet. If I need something, I have a clerk that keeps a copy of every memo. All I have to do is pick up the phone and ask her to look up something for me. I no longer fill up my home with tons of papers that I will never look at again.

For my mother's bills (I am responsible for them), I keep every receipt. I use a briefcase and an accordion alphabet file. It is portable and I use it with her social workers and doctors at times. I have to keep the bills until her estate is settled.

15. **Family pictures**

This is a problem we all have. Some people have drawers full of pictures that are unlabeled. We have all seen old pictures in our mother's home that we could not identify. This is so sad. My Mom did one thing that was very nice. She had a scrapbook for each of our family members with our history in it. Newspaper pictures, snapshots, school pictures, and report cards. Don't start doing this until all your clutter is under control. You will get sidetracked. You will have time for pleasure when the clutter is gone. I promise.

16. **Birth Certificates / Marriage Certificate / Passports /**
   Death Certificates / Divorce Papers / Adoption Papers

These all need to be protected in a fireproof safe or a bank lock box. Make copies to keep at home so you will have them when you need them, but keep the originals in a safe place. A place to keep them at home: in a notebook with sheet protectors or in a file labeled "Important Family Records." Also, savings bonds need to be kept in a lock box.

17. **Purses full of STUFF**

Each week clean out your purse. Most of what is in there is trash. You might even find some money. I clean out my purse on Fridays.

18. **Maps**

You have old maps in your car from the 80s. Did you know that they are just about ready to fall apart? Get rid of them. Buy a new one for your state or go to your local County Commissioner's office and get a copy of your state's latest DOT map.

19. **Travel brochures**

We have all of these places we want to go, but the brochures are 10 years old. Get rid of them. The prices are outdated as well as the phone numbers. Make a list of the places you would like to see and look them up on the Internet.

20. **Organizational books**

Put your organizational books away. There is no way you can follow several programs at one time. Pick one and stick to it. If you choose FlyLady, then put the other ones away. A hound dog cannot catch eight rabbits at one time, she has to pick one and stay focused.

21. 3 x 5 cards

If you use Pam and Peggy's (*Sidetracked Home Executives*) 3 x 5 card file system and you have not used them in a long time, it is time to toss them too. I used my old card file system to develop my routines. Then I got rid of my guilt.

22. Other office supplies and addictions

File folders and dividers. We all have lots of this stuff. I have one drawer for my office supplies. This takes up part of one of my empty drawers in my filing cabinet.

You all have been asking for paperwork clutter-problem solutions. I hope I have touched on this subject. Keep in mind that these problems are not going to get fixed overnight, but you can stop them from piling up by dealing with your mail as soon as it comes to your home, throwing away the trash and only keeping what you will need. Toss the rest.

Watch your back for paper clutter. It attacks all the time.

Dear FlyLady...

DON'T DROWN IN PAPER

I just had an AHA moment. I thought for sure that I was too young in FlyBaby time to have one. But your e-mails about the paper clutter really hit home. I have been preaching the simple way and the removal of clutter and the 'less is more' idea for years. I have blamed my DH for keeping us in clutter. Then you brought up paper clutter. I saw my desk overflowing with papers and my filing cabinet stuffed with papers. MY DESK! This was not my husband's doing. It was mine. Somewhere, I got the idea that I needed to save all those papers. I believed we had to "document" everything to protect ourselves from harm. I began tracking everything ... paid bills, receipts, bank statements ... Why? In all the time I have done this, I can't remember ever having to actually USE any of it. I can see now that the paper wasn't protecting us ... it was drowning us ... Thank you, FlyLady, for showing me that I can let go of my guilt and purge this clutter.

—Joelle from Minnesota

Menus — What's for Supper?

How many times have you stood in front of your refrigerator at suppertime and not had a clue what you are going to feed your family? All of us struggle with preparing meals and it becomes such a chore because we don't plan ahead. I know you are tired of having to run to the grocery store any time you begin to cook. Part of FLYing is knowing "What's for Supper!"

We have devised a generic plan to help you stay ahead of the feeding game if you will follow these simple instructions. First you have to set aside a time each week to do your menu planning and put together a grocery list before you go to the market. I guarantee you will be seeing less of the pizza man and those fast food franchises. This alone will relieve you of so much guilt that you will be FLYing all the way to the bank with the money you have saved from doing menu planning.

Here is how Menu Planning works:

1. I want you to get a big calendar with large blocks. Every day write down what you have for supper in the block, even if you eat out. This will be the beginning of your favorite menus.

2. Think of the main dishes for each day of the week. Kind of like a skeleton for the week.

Here is mine:

Sunday	Miscellaneous (on your own) or chicken
Monday	Beef
Tuesday	Pasta/casserole
Wednesday	Pork
Thursday	Soup and salad or stew (Crock-Pot meal)
Friday	Special dinner/eat out /or fix romantic meal
Saturday	Pizza

You could have other options: soup and sandwiches, fish, ethnic night, kids' favorites, family favorites, or "Try a New Recipe Night."

3. I want you to brainstorm for a little while. Under each category take a stack of 3x5s and list the entrée of your meal. That is all. Set a timer for 15 minutes and write down as many side dishes as you can think of that your family enjoys. Then you have to stop. Do not get sidetracked by this. Then you can add the side dishes to the card. There is nothing worse than having a chicken thawed and nothing to go with it. Write it down so you don't have to think about it.

4. Do not come up with strange recipes. You will not fix them. Only list the tried and true meals that you all love. There will be time for experimental meals later.

5. Also, make a list of the meals your family loves for special occasions: birthdays, anniversaries, graduation. List the meals that you eat at restaurants. This is not hard, so don't make this difficult. Only work on it for 15 minutes. Do not go into perfectionist mode.

A Fully Stocked Pantry Takes Time to Fill

My pantry is fully stocked for almost every meal I cook. Sometimes I have two of each item so I only need to replace what I have used up. This keeps me from making several trips to the grocery store and my shopping is so much easier with my hectic schedule. This did not happen overnight. It took several months of buying a little here and there to stock our pantry.

Each time I went shopping I would buy the ingredients for a meal. I would buy two of everything, especially things that we used often. I would freeze bread and other things. Another place to purchase bulk food is the restaurant supply store. You can get flour, pasta, beans, olive oil, and almost anything at these places. This was a wonderful way to buy staples in bulk. I bought empty lard tins to store the food in and put some of the dried beans in the freezer.

Some of you are still struggling with your daily routines. I throw this out for those that are ready to tackle the menu monster and pantry. We all can do this, but the routines will free us up to be able to think about more than just housework. If you are not ready to deal with the pantry/menu planning, that is fine. Take BabySteps and this will happen before you know it. One day you will be standing in your clean home and ask yourself, "What am I going to do now?"

I have a whole wall of shelves in the basement that I use as a pantry. This is wonderful. I don't have to have all of that in my tiny kitchen. Once you declutter your home you will find storage areas that you never thought about. Your food pantry can be anywhere.

Be creative: hall closets, bathroom vanities, or under end tables.

Think about this. You don't have to do this just yet, let it in and roll it around for a while. You will be FLY-Washed before you know it.

Grocery List

I have a list that contains everything we buy at the grocery store. The list is broken down into grocery sections. It took a little while to develop, but I keep a copy in my Control Journal and just highlight what we are running low on. You can either put it in a sheet protector or print out a bunch of them so all you do is grab your list and go. It is worth your time to come up with your own list for your family's wants and needs. I also have one for household supplies that I buy at a discount store.

"This next testimonial just goes to show you what happens when you make an appointment with yourself to meal plan or anything that you need to set as a priority. If you don't have a basic weekly plan, think about this message and decide for yourself what is holding you back. A little planning can save a ton of money."

Dear FlyLady...

PLANNING SAVES MONEY

Hi FlyLady and FlyBabies,

I just wanted to say that menu planning has been a big payoff for me. I run my own in-home show decorating and gift business and my busy season has begun so I am away from home more now. Before, I had to worry about what to fix for the evening meal if I was out late into the afternoon; or if I had to go out that evening and didn't have the meal thought of, much less fixed, I would run to the fast food or to a grocery deli for the meal. Well, now by having a planned menu I am not running like a crazy chicken. I know what I am fixing and most of the time the items are waiting on the counter by the stove or if frozen, in the refrigerator thawing with a note on counter that it's in refrigerator thawing. That way if DH wants to start cooking he knows what to fix and can get it started with NO STRESS for either of us. But what I found by having planned menus was a lot of extra benefits that have saved me time and money. I would like to share these with you.

1. By having a menu there's no worry or waste of time wondering what you're going to fix.

2. A menu helps save money because you don't just throw things on the stove to cook or fix something someone does not eat and then you have to throw away. (For example, my DH likes whole kernel corn, I like beets. By having a menu I can plan for this and buy the small single serving size and even though it may be a few cents more I am saving money because there is nothing to throw away.)

3. By having a menu, you fix just what is going to be eaten so you don't have any leftovers, which helps keep the refrigerator cleaner.

4. By having a menu you are preparing better choices of food and are being nicer to your health and well-being.

I thought before that I didn't have time to make up a menu plan, but now I have come to realize that by taking 15 minutes to do this I save myself lots of time and stress so I can do other, more fun things or just have ME time.

Thank you again!

Cheryl from Tennessee

PLANNING SAVES TIME

Hi! I just got back from my weekly shopping at the Commissary. I had such a wonderful time … I just had to let you know. Since you sent out the message this morning about pantry stocking and menu planning, I thought I would thank you, since menu planning has changed my life. BMP (before meal planning), my trips to the grocery store were hectic. The commissary is usually very busy … not the ideal environment for planning meals in my head. I knew that planning my menu in advance was the best strategy. Now when I get there, I know exactly what I want: I have a meal for each day imagined, and ingredients listed. Shopping goes seven times quicker, and is actually fun. Amazing what a little planning beforehand can do to liberate time later!

Amy from Okinawa, Japan

Vacation: Plan Ahead—
Don't Lose Your Head

Is getting ready to leave on vacation a pain in the bottom to you?

Do you run around like your head is cut off for several days prior to your departure time, not knowing which way to turn?

Are you irritable and snapping at your loved ones?

Do you pack everything but the kitchen sink?

This is a characteristic of a SHE. I have done this so many times. Several years ago it would take me two weeks to pack for a two-week vacation. In the end I was so exhausted, I just wanted to crash. So, I have some tips for you.

SIT DOWN with a pen and paper and PLAN! Fifteen minutes of planning gets rid of the "chicken with the head cut off" syndrome! Break your list into four parts or use four separate pages.

1. Things to do before you pack.

2. Things you will need to pack.

3. Things to do before you leave.

4. Things to do when you get home.

1. The things you will need to do before you pack are:

- Make sure all of your clothes are clean and put away.
- The house is in good order, everything in its place.
- Make a grocery list of food to take with you and buy it.
- Take care of your pets' needs — get a sitter or arrange for boarding — and their food. (This will be out of the way.)
- Notify the post office that you will be out of town and to hold your mail, or ask a trusted person to pick up your mail and newspapers.
- Do you have the directions printed out from MapQuest and in your planner?
- Get car serviced and filled up if you are going in the car.
- If you are flying, make sure your tickets are in order and in your planner or purse.
- What time do you need to be at the airport?
- What time do you need to leave the house to get to the airport on time?

2. Things you need to pack:

- Each family member gets a 3 x 5 inch card. On this card I list everything that needs to be packed for that person, such as a favorite toy, golf clubs, fishing gear, clothes, and favorite snack.
- Make a card that is labeled: Food to Take.
- Decide upon the outfits for each person.
  Be sure to check your itinerary for places where you will need dress clothes — church, fancy restaurants, etc. Don't forget bathing suits, beach towels, and beach shoes. If you don't have access to a washer, you may have to pack an outfit for each day, unless the kids are going to be in their bathing suits all day. Then you will need to take a couple of them.
- Plan your clothes. Keep it simple; mix and match your out-

fits, then you will have less to take. Keep your makeup and hair care items to a bare minimum. Don't forget a hat and sunscreen if you are going to be outside a lot. How about a book or magazine to read?

- Assist your husband. Sometimes he needs to pack for himself, but make a list just in case and double check. He will be happy you are looking out for his needs, too.
- Don't forget medications and a small first aid kit. I would put all of this stuff in one bag, called my "bathroom bag."
- Bags: My rule of thumb is one medium bag per person, plus a "mother bag" to take care of odds and ends (i.e., carry-on tote).

3. Things to do before you leave:

- Set your FlyLady Mentors' e-mail up on web only. E-mail me if you need me to do it for you.
- Change all the sheets. Do that so when you get home your bed is nice and welcoming. I do this the day before I leave. There is no time when you are leaving early in the morning.
- Make sure the house is clean and sparkling, so when you walk in the door you are not blown away by a messy house.
- Put disinfectant in each of your toilets and pour a little in your drains. Use something you like to smell. This will keep your house from smelling bad due to stagnant water. If you leave pets in the house, put the lids down on the toilet.
- Throw the breaker for the hot water heater if you are going to be gone for two or more weeks.
- Turn the air conditioner up to about 85 degrees or completely off. In winter, turn your heat up to at least 45 degrees so the pipes don't freeze.
- Check your freezer to make sure the door is closed. Don't ask

me why I do this, all I will tell you is it is not fun to come home to a freezer full of spoiled food. Then tape it shut.

4. Make a note of the things to do when you get home and leave it on the kitchen counter.

- Turn on air conditioner or heat and water heater.
- Unpack car as soon as you get home or it could be weeks before it is done.
- Start a load of laundry when you get the suitcases in the house, before you crash. I make sure my bags are unpacked as soon as I walk in the door. If I don't, I will be living out of my suitcase for another week.
- Reset your e-group FlyLady Mentors' e-mail to your setting.

Now start your week over just like it was Sunday afternoon. Make out your Basic Weekly Plan. Life is back to normal. Don't forget your routines! Now is not the time to fall off the routine wagon.

So it's time to jump back in and start over. Put this stuff on the Return Home note on your kitchen counter. That way you will not have to remember it and it will be just like you are being bossed around by someone.

I know this looks like a lot to do. But these are things you already know about. When they are in black and white they are not as scary.

Now you have a plan. Whenever you need to get ready for a trip, drag this out and use it. Put it in your planner for just those occasions. Put the lists in a sheet protector and slide the note cards in with them. That way you will not have to reinvent the wheel each time you travel. You will just need to adjust for your destination.

Have a great vacation and don't forget to take some time for yourself.

Some packing tips:

This packing list was based on one by my dear friend and very first FlyBaby, Pam Kuczora, when she stayed in a condo at the beach. I've included blank items so you can fill in your own additions to the list.

BASIC PACKING LIST

ARRANGEMENTS

____ask a neighbor to bring in mail and newspapers for recycling

____make arrangements for petsitter or boarding

____clean out pet cages or kennel

____pack pet's food, treats, leash, etc.

____

____

____

CLOTHES

____changes of clothes

____sets of underwear (underpants, socks, undershirts, bras, slips, jockstraps)

____sleep shirts/pajamas

____dress outfits (pantyhose/tights)

____shoes (tennis, sandals, dress, slippers)

____robes (bath, swim coverups)

____special sports clothes (tennis, golf, skiing)

____swimsuits

____swim towels

____goggles, swimmies

____sweatsuits

____sweaters

____jackets

____heavy coats, mittens, hats, boots

____

____

____

TOILETRIES

____toothbrushes

____toothpaste

____deodorant

____hairbrush

____hair things

____shampoo

____kids' shampoo

____bubble bath

____lotion

____bug spray

____sun block

____chapstick

____medications: Synthroid, Lactaid, Tylenol, Pediacare,
    Tums, vitamins, cough syrup

____nail file

____contacts/case/solutions

____shaving kit

____makeup bag

____

____

____

FOOD

____water

____lidded cups

____bowls, spoons

____peanut butter

____knife, spoon

____cereal

____milk

____raisins

____paper towels

____tissues

____kitchen disinfectant

____aroma candle

____napkins

____wet wipes

____crackers

____bread

____cheese

____soda

____

____

____

MISCELLANEOUS

____pillows

____sleeping bags

____cell phone, cord, and charger

____stamps, pen, paper

____hostess gift(s)

____map(s)

TRAVEL INFO

____reservation forms

____reservation number

____resort information

____maps

____

____

____

ENTERTAINMENT

____books (Bible, fiction, etc.)

____magazines

____games, cards

____journal

____handwork (quilt, embroidery, knitting, etc.)

____videos

____cassettes/CDs

____sporting equipment (tennis racquets, balls, pool toys, etc.)

____

____

____

LAST MINUTE

____feed and leave water for cat, or any other pets staying home

____change litter

____take dog to kennel

____set VCR(s)

____turn on porch light, set timers

____clear answering machine

____water plants

____check doors, turn all appliances off

____turn down heat/air conditioning

____postcard labels and postcard stamps

____gather bills that will be due while you're gone

____bring sufficient checks to pay bills

____large garbage bags for dirty clothes

____laundry soap

____fabric softener

____

____

____

**"Bon Voyage!
Don't forget to have
a FUN trip!"**

Dear FlyLady...

READY TO LEAVE AT A MOMENT'S NOTICE

Dear FlyLady,

Usually going on vacation brings mixed feelings. The relief of getting away from my mess always felt great, but the guilt of leaving the mess and ESPECIALLY coming back to the mess, was awful. Imagine sitting on a glorious beach full of DREAD, because the next day you have to return to the CHAOS.

A weekend get-away, not to mention a last minute get-away, was basically out of the question. How could I leave the sink full of dirty dishes, the piles of junk, the unmade beds, and the pile of laundry? Speaking of laundry, how could I pack for a spontaneous trip when all my family's clothes were dirty and scattered everywhere?

Well, I've been FLYing for 3 months now, and about an hour ago, my husband came home from work early and said, "How would you like to go away for the weekend, and how would you like to leave in an hour?" It was so easy to say "YES!!!" My dishes were running in the dishwasher at that very moment, the beds were made, all our clothes were clean and folded in the drawers, I have a CLEAN HOUSE!

My husband is packing the car right now, and my toddler is SO excited to be going on a "twip." I can't thank you enough for all you do!

Without you my life would be full of stress right now, but instead I am just full of excitement!

My DH is honking the horn, so off we go!
Thank you from the bottom of my heart,
Ashley from Tennessee

THERE'S NO PLACE LIKE HOME

Dear FlyLady,

I will never be able to find the words to thank you for what your system has done for me and my family. I am a home schooling mother of five who always felt I was three steps behind where I should be. My home overwhelmed me and every other home I went to always seemed to be happier, cozier, more beautiful than mine. But things have changed. I realized just how much when we took a weekend trip to N.E. Georgia to see the change of leaves this past fall. We rented a cabin in the mountains. The minute I walked in I was amazed. The cabin was beautifully decorated, everything was immaculate. The beds were covered with warm clean quilts. The kitchen was uncluttered and sparkled. The living room was decorated simply but with great taste.

In the past I would have wished my home could be just like it but what went through my mind instead was "Wow, this feels just like home." My eight year old came running from outside and said, "Mom, this looks just like our house." Without even knowing it, tears ran down my face. I was so happy to find I had what I always wanted. So let me thank you from the bottom of my heart for what you have done. You have a mission and someday you will come to know just how many people you have helped.

May God bless you and those who help you with your mission always!

FlyBaby C from Florida

Moving —You Don't Have to Panic!

Every week we have several members that holler *HELP!*

"We are moving and I don't know where to start. We have to put this house up for sale and it is awful. Please tell me what to do!!"

"We are moving cross-country and I don't know where to start packing."

"When we move, I don't know how I can unpack and keep the chaos of the move from overwhelming me."

These are some hard situations, but I have a simple answer.
(a) BABYSTEPS! YES, YOU HEARD ME RIGHT. WE HAVE TO BREAK THE JOB DOWN INTO SMALLER PARTS.
(b) DON'T MOVE ANYTHING YOU DON'T LOVE!

With our SHE mentality, when we look at the whole picture we become overwhelmed and paralyzed. This is just how we are made, but I can give you some simple rules to follow. As SHEs, we usually wait until the very last minute to start doing anything. I can hear you now: "I work better under pressure!" NO YOU DON'T! IT MAKES YOU SICK AND THAT IS THE LAST THING YOU NEED WHEN YOU ARE TRYING TO MOVE AND UNPACK AND TAKE CARE OF A FAMILY ON TOP OF IT ALL.

I know the thought of moving is more than you can handle right now! For some of you, moving is done every year. That in itself is a reason to declutter your homes. If you have been in the same house for 20 years and you have never thought

"If you don't love it, don't move it."

about packing up all your stuff, then you are going to have an eye-opening experience. If you will wrap your brain around this, then you may be able to release your clutter so you won't have to pay for the shipping of your trash to your new home. Another reason to play this game is to declutter your home so your children won't have to someday.

I can just hear your adult babies now, "Why in the world did Momma save this?!"

On the 27th of every month we pretend that we are going to put our home on the real estate market. This is a game, but many of you have been faced with this because you have to move. I want to make this transition easier.

Homework assignment: Realtor Missions

Put on a different hat — look through someone else's eyes.

1. Pretend to be a realtor. Your job is to tell the homeowner what needs to be done to make the house look better before it goes on the market.

2. Get your notebook or clipboard and walk through the house.

3. Look at each room, starting at the front door and working clockwise throughout the house.

4. Look at everything and write it down. This does not mean that you are going to have to do all of this. The list will be your master list and you will be incorporating a few of these items as we work through our zones next month. You will list items such as painting; new carpet; new curtains; decluttering jobs, such as cleaning out the closet, under the bed — anything that comes to mind. I don't care if you can't afford it. Just list the item. This is a want list and a to-do list all in one.

5. After you finish, put it in your Control Journal where you are keeping your routines. Each week we will look at the list and get our dreams in our heads. We will also incorporate some of the cleaning items into our zones. This is not hard; it will take you 10 minutes. Do it like you have another appointment shortly. Don't think too much about this. It does not have to be typed, Ms. Perfectionist.

Visualize your home as a comfortable, huggable refuge for your family. Think happy thoughts. You will get there, I promise. It is all a process. Next month we will look at the old list and see if any of it got done. I love this part. Because you don't even know you have done it until you check it off in the next month. Celebrate!

Moving Out

1. I want you to breathe first, then get a note pad and start to make a plan. We jump into a project like this helter-skelter without taking a few minutes to just think about it.

2. For every recipe you need a list of ingredients. So think about what you are going to use for the job.

Boxes

These can be purchased at a moving supply company, U-Haul, Ryder, United Van Lines, Mayflower, etc. These folks sell used boxes at a reduced rate. You can also go to liquor stores for their empty boxes. Keep in mind that you do not need to get huge boxes because they will be hard to lift when filled. So keep them manageable. If you have boxes with boxtop flaps, you will need to seal them.

Packing tape

Be sure and get plenty of this stuff. It is not that expensive and it is worth having enough so you don't have to stop and run out to buy more. Also, get the dispensers to hold the tape and have more than one if there will be other people helping pack.

Scissors

If you don't get the dispensers, you will need scissors. Just remember, they are hard to keep up with while you are packing.

Garbage bags

Preferably use the kind that you can see through. That way you will not have to reopen them to see if it is trash or something you packed that would not fit in a box. Get very strong ones. Code them with colored ribbons.

Colored markers

I use colored ones so that I can give each room a different color. That way, when we are unloading the truck, all I have to say is, "Yellow boxes go in the kitchen, green in this bedroom, purple in the living room." Then you can post the color of the boxes over the top of the doorway to that room. Be sure the color code matches the ribbon tied around the garbage bags. Stickers and markers usually don't work on them because they either fall off or you can't see them. Clothes are usually in these bags, so raid your sewing stash for old ribbon or your Christmas stash for Christmas ribbon. It is cheap and easy to recognize.

Decide ahead of time what your color codes are going to be and put those supplies in the room. Just don't label all the boxes, 'Miscellaneous'! You can also give them a number and put the contents of that box on your note pad so that you can find items that you need without tearing open each and every box and creating even more CHAOS!

Labeling

As far as labeling the boxes: If you start packing up the things that you least need and start at 1 and label in ascending order, you will know that the boxes with the lowest numbers can be unpacked last. The higher-numbered boxes are the ones with the stuff you use most.

Newspapers

This is for packing your dishes and other breakable items. You can never have enough newspapers.

Getting the house ready to sell

This is usually a precursor to the big move. Right now, you are so overwhelmed with the clutter that you don't know where to start.

This may sound like a drastic move, but if you can afford it, order a dumpster. It will give you a place to put things, or call for daily pick up from the area thrift/charity stores. You just have to get the STUFF out of your house as fast as you can. I don't want you to attack this problem without thinking a little about this.

If you run around like your head was cut off, you are not going to be accomplishing anything. So start in one room. You can even start to pack up the stuff you will not be needing at the same time. Pick up an item and ask yourself, "Are you worth moving, do I love you enough to go to all this trouble and expense to pack you up, or should you rather have a new home and save me time and effort?" You are going to be so surprised at how much stuff you can actually do without. This is the key to getting the house ready to put on the market. Once you get rid of the clutter that is making your home too small, you may not even have to sell. This has happened!

Keep only the stuff you absolutely love and use regularly.

Get rid of all the clothes you don't wear, too.

Now, back to packing:

If you will take your time and not be rushed about this, you will do a more efficient job and not be so stressed out. Do you hear me on this? I do not want you to make yourself sick. Slow and steady wins the race — not crash and burn!

If you have plenty of time to prepare for the move, you can have everything labeled and ready to load on the truck before the final day. No stress and no worry. Also, you will be able to find things when you get to your new home. Take BabySteps and each day pack up five boxes and keep them in the room that they belong in. Color code the boxes and number them. Label the contents or the drawer they came from on the outside and put it on your master moving list. Get a clipboard to keep everything together or a zip-up notebook or canvas bag to hold all your markers and supplies. Keep your moving supplies together. If you have to do this by yourself, you will thank me later.

Moving into your new dream home

Now let's talk about what you are going to need when you get to the new house. I don't want you ripping open boxes looking for things. So, here is what you are going to do first before you start to pack anything. Think about what items you are going to need when you walk in the door of the house.

Cleaning supplies

Rubber gloves for cleaning the bathroom. I know I may be funny, but these were someone else's germs, not your family's. Disinfectant: Lysol, Pine Sol, Comet, Windex. You may need to clean before you can unpack. So you may have to race the movers to the new house. Rags and paper towels for cleaning.

Vacuum, broom, mop

I know you may not use them, but you will need to know where to put your hands on them as soon as the movers have finished unloading the truck.

Basic kitchen utensils

A skillet, a pot, a coffee pot, maybe even your Crock-Pot. Then a spatula, sharp knife, silverware, dishwashing liquid, dish towels, paper plates, napkins, glasses.

Simple food

Peanut butter, cereal, crackers, bread, coffee, sugar, powdered milk. (I have to have this for coffee.) I can also use it on cereal in a pinch. You may have to make a grocery run for some fruit and snacks for the kids.

Clothes

You will need a couple of changes of clothes for each person in the family, everything from underwear to socks, shoes, and pajamas.

A basic bathroom bag

Everyone's toothbrushes, razor, shampoo, soap, toothpaste and, of course, toilet paper and towels and washcloths. Don't forget your makeup, hair dryer, and contact stuff. You don't want be tearing open boxes, hunting for this stuff, when you are getting ready to crash into bed with mattresses on the floor. Also pack some sheets and blankets for each person's bed and an alarm clock. This should be just enough to help with camping out while you are working on getting the house put back together.

Don't forget:

A phone and plug-in cord, your packing supply bag with garbage bags, and your inventory and special labels that you have made for each doorway so the movers will know where to put the boxes without you standing at the front door directing traffic. I can just see you now. "This goes over there. What does that box say?" I want you to let the workmen do the work so you can start cleaning and unpacking your kitchen as it comes in the door, especially the food that you may have moved. (Oh, by the way, if you are moving frozen food, you will need good ice chests to pack it in. I recommend using it all up before the move or giving it to your old neighbors before you leave. I would start over with fresh stuff for your refrigerator. Toss it all out, except the mustard. That doesn't need to be refrigerated.)

Before you leave the old house, make sure the power and phone are on at the new house. This way you will literally not be in the dark. Also, think about having a cleaning service come and clean the old house for you. Your attentions are not there anymore. Let someone else do it for you. The realtor can even hire someone for you.

When the moving truck gets there, you will need to be the director. Have the children stationed in their rooms so as to be out of the way unless they are big enough to fetch and tote. Tell them not to start dragging out their stuff until their furniture is in the room and they have a place to put their clothes. Have them put the boxes against one wall and warn them about not trying to climb on top of them. You have your hands full. You don't need a trip to the emergency room from a busted noggin.

Main rule here

As you unpack it, put it where it goes, break down the boxes, and throw away the paper. Do not start another box until everything is put away. I don't want you to handle it twice.

First meal

You are going to have to feed this hungry mob, too. So either plan on going out for take-out or throwing something in your Crock Pot. You can get creative with this one if you want. Toss in a roast, a package of Lipton Onion Soup Mix, and a bag of baby carrots and some new potatoes. Or you can make canned spaghetti sauce and boil up some pasta with some French bread. You could even pack a tablecloth and spread it over some boxes for a picnic dinner. What a memory! Your first real meal in your new home. But I will understand if you just go get take out.

Getting back into a routine

The next day is when your head starts going crazy. You have so much to do and you don't know where to start. I can tell you exactly where to begin. You start your morning routine. Yes, you heard me right. I want you to get up that first morning in your new and wonderful home and get yourself dressed to shoes, hair, and face, and then, as you get ready, start picking up after yourself. Head to the kitchen and start breakfast.

While you are sitting having your breakfast, do not look at how much you have to do, only concentrate on making a list of the most important things to do first. That will keep your home running smoothly.

Miscellaneous tasks:

- Get the washer and dryer hooked up.
- Get the dishwasher running.
- Buy groceries for the family. Make out a list. Or, if you have an initial grocery shopping list that you made while you were doing your planning, grab it from your moving notebook.
- Put on something for supper, or at least have some idea about what to fix.

Now you have a plan and can begin to unpack. After you take care of your priorities you can start to unpack one box at a time. Only do five, then stop and rest. You may want to go to the next room and do five boxes in there; just rotate around the house putting things away. Remember, as you unpack things, if you don't have a place for it, you may not need it. So do not just start putting those things in a pile. Decide where it should go and don't put off making that decision until you have a whole room filled with your indecision.

I want this move to be peaceful. It can be if you take it slow and steady and do not stress out. You did not get packed up and moved in a day and you are not going to have the house put back together in a day. If your husband thinks that can happen, you tell him to talk to me. I want you to stick to your plan and take BabySteps unpacking. After you have the basic household items unpacked, just take five boxes a day and put things away where you want them to go. Toss out what you really don't love or need and put the things you do love in their new home.

This move can be a clutter-clearing experience if you take it step by step. You can do this. All you have to do is have a plan and follow your plan. Do not try to unpack in your gown and slippers.

I want your new home to radiate the love you have for yourself.

MOVING TIPS FROM OUR MEMBERS:

We have gotten some wonderful tips to add to my essay on moving. Check them out:

THINGS TO THINK ABOUT FIRST...

1. Our move was a short distance and for the clothes, we took the drawers out of the dressers, carried the dressers to the truck, then replaced the drawers. It's not a good way to get rid of clutter, but it's easier than packing clothes neatly. This is good for a do-it-yourself move — professional movers probably wouldn't do it.

2. Here is my tip about moving / decluttering:

Instead of the expensive ($400 / week in my town) dumpster for serious decluttering, we rented a UHaul truck ($30). We had put all the trash including trash furniture into the garage. That took about four days. We then rented the truck for one day, loaded it up, and drove (with our kids to help) to the dump. There we were able to unload all that trash for free. And there were a couple of people there who were picking through our stuff as soon as we unloaded. They were taking old furniture (even broken furniture). I guess it's true that one man's trash is another man's treasure. That was a BIG savings! Oh, I did have to go buy some work gloves for the kids (another $24).

3. I moved three times in a year before we moved into the new home we built, and two locations were furnished condos . After living with someone else's few household supplies, I very quickly came to realize what I really needed, missed of my own (cookbooks and ceramic mugs), and could very easily do without. While we were planning the move, I laid out my kitchen, planning the most convenient location for dishes, silverware, pots & pans, etc. to make unpacking easier. Shortly after the movers left, I put down my plan and began unpacking the kitchen. I had my cabinet for plastics all set up (I had to buy a few things in the condo) and was happily unpacking when I came upon a dishes box (they're pretty big and tall). It was full of plastics — dozens of souvenir cups, warped and stained containers, containers with missing lids, and more! I sorted through the box, keeping only the containers I really used and liked (just a few) and took the rest to Goodwill. It was so nice to have a plastics cupboard that I could actually use without digging through for mates.

4. Another tip for moving-out-day and moving-in-day is to purchase a simple little apron with big pockets. I bought mine in the painting area at WalMart. It has two large pockets so you can carry around your markers, precut pieces of ribbon, your notebook (if it's small enough), or a smaller notebook that you can make notes in and transfer to your larger notebook. They have these as a waist type and the type that hang from your neck and tie around your waist.

5. Here's a tip that will work especially well for those moving out of rented homes, but may also work for those selling: Pack only what you want to move and then invite Goodwill, or whomever, in and say, "Whatever you want, take." They'll bring a truck and move it all out including clothes, furniture, whatever. What's left will be mostly

trash and a few things you can take to a drop-off place. I haven't tried this, but it's what I'm going to do when we leave here!

6. Another tip specifically for those of you in the military, PLEASE ask housing about the moving allowance!! It is a little more hassle but works wonderfully! They give you an itemized household contents list to fill out, which gives you a great chance to do some 27 Fling Boogie-ing! Having to write that you have six years of magazines with dust on them ... well, you get the idea! By going through housing, they WILL reimburse you for your expenses, including U-Hauls, meals, and hotel rooms en-route to your new duty station, plus you get a standard bonus for moving yourself. (Ours totaled up to almost $2000.) That way you can itemize your home contents and get back the money you spend on your supplies. You must be diligent about receipts, though, so get a folder for them! Happy moving!

7. Hi, I just moved and I was in luck when I asked at church if anyone knew of any boxes. I found a family that had just been moved by their company and I got Mayflower moving boxes free! Even the wonderful wardrobe ones. I also went to a business that I was a regular customer at and asked for packing material. I was able to get all kinds of bubble wrap, white packing paper, and peanuts. I went to the newspaper printer and was able to buy 10 pounds of unprinted newspaper on the roll for $10.00. I had more than enough. You are right about the tape; you do need lots of it.

8. Pictures with glass. Always wrap separately and pack so they are standing as they hang. DO NOT LAY FLAT!!!!

9. Pack the boxes solid. Even if you have to fill in with crumbled paper or peanuts. This keeps them from collapsing. What a mess if

the bottom of the stack of boxes collapses. By solid, I mean that nothing shakes or slides around in the box.

10. I gave away a bunch of my stuff when we last moved. One of the local nonprofit groups with a thrift store had a particular day each week when they would come to my zip code. They probably thought I was nuts, but I had them put me on the schedule for weeks. The fellows who picked up the usable items would just laugh when they ended up at my house again!

Also, I rented a U-Haul trailer. Spending money when I had a perfectly good old pickup truck to haul things with goes against my nature, but a local rental wasn't too bad and it gives you a covered, protected place to put your giveaways as you sort.

11. One thing that helped me tremendously during moving was a timer. At the time I was totally addicted to chatting on BBS (before internet) and it was almost impossible to drag myself away from the keyboard. (I was so bad I'd DREAM about chatting, wake up typing on my pillow, haha!) Anyway, I started packing early so I'd have plenty of time. I'd allow myself 30 minutes chatting, 30 minutes packing, 30 minutes chatting, 30 minutes packing … You know how much you can get done in 5, 10, or 15 minutes already … I got most of the essentials (books, china, decorations, etc) packed in a very short time and stacked out of the way against a wall. It was one of the easiest moves that I can remember, clutter and all! Next time, definitely a 27 Fling Boogie beforehand! :)

BOXES

1. To get boxes, look in the Yellow Pages under "Boxes." That's what

I did, and I got them cheaper than from either U-Haul or the moving company, and the guy delivered them right to the house.

2. Check with your local pharmacy for boxes if you can't afford to buy new ones. The boxes the vials come in are a great size for books and most other things. And the pharmacy will also get boxes from time to time that are divided for glass bottles (you can pack your glasses in there, and smaller knick-knacks).

3. Every time we move (and it's been quite often as of late) we go to the local bookstore or liquor store and ask if we can raid their cardboard dumpster. They almost always have a separate dumpster just for the cardboard, and the boxes are usually collapsed so you can fit more of them in the car. These boxes are very sturdy. They are usually medium-sized boxes and are easy to carry when packed. The best part is they're FREE!

4. Go to the grocery store for banana boxes. They are a great size, the top fits down completely over the bottom, and they have handles!

5. We moved recently and a new neighbor was getting ready to move away. Judy took over a bunch of our boxes (especially the dish crates and wardrobe boxes) and the packing paper. Yes, it may have taken me a moment longer to flatten/fold the paper rather than squash it but …. So keep an eye out for someone moving in (especially if it is a government or other employer-paid move — our professional packers were VERY generous in their use of boxes and paper). A plate of cookies or a casserole for your new neighbor just might provide you with more boxes than you can deal with!

PACKING PAPER

1. If you can get it, the plain newsprint style paper is worth it. Why?! With newspaper, you'll be covered with newsprint. It comes off your hands onto the doors, the cabinets, the walls, your dishes, the bisque figurine you got when your grandma passed away, your face, your kids, etc. Moving is stressful enough, we FlyKids don't need any more stress.

2. I always wrap dishes in plastic wrap, before padding with news-paper. That way they don't get ink on them and can be put away once the paper is removed and the ink is washed off my hands, and I don't have to pay for unprinted newsprint.

3. A while back, I found that I was moving every year. Instead of newspaper or any paper for wrapping breakables, I would use my towels and clothes to do this. The clothes were good for laying in between plates and dishes. And as I unpacked, I just refolded and put everything into its proper drawers and shelves.

4. I recommend paper plates between the dishes! They cushion them wonderfully! And you can still use them afterwards!

5. Here is another tip from a military wife who has definitely been there! I use my bath towels as padding for my breakable stuff. Once we arrive, as we finish unpacking each box, I use the time to weed out the old ratty towels and TOSS THEM! Since the bathroom has always been the FIRST place I get set up (obvious reasons) this towel purge gives me a chance to go from an unpacked room into a finished room, and gives me HOPE that I will get it all done!

Dear FlyLady...

FLYING HELPED SELL MY HOME

FlyLady & Kelly,

I have to thank you from the bottom of my heart for your Realtor Missions!!!

Allow me to back up a few months. DH and I have been casually looking for a home in our area with some acreage. We found a home that we liked and wanted to make an offer. We have a new baby (he was 3 months old at that time) and I was absolutely terrified at the thought of putting up an offer and being forced to put my home on the market in a hurry. Fortunately that home didn't pass inspections, and we didn't purchase it. But it got me thinking about Kelly's Realtor Missions. I decided to do one (baby was 4 months at this point), so I walked each room and made a list. DH and I have casually made repairs in our free time and I have used the zones to declutter each room and do heavier cleaning (i.e, windows etc.). Anyhow to make a long story short ... 2 weeks ago we found the perfect house and our offer was accepted!! Our offer was accepted on a Friday, and I was able to stick a sign in my yard and host an Open house THAT SAME WEEKEND ON SUNDAY!!! All it took was doing my Weekly Home Blessing a few days early. I am still in a state of shock about how easy it was to host that Open House. I had several people comment that my home looked like a magazine ad because it was so clean and decluttered. My neighbors commented that I hadn't been married long enough to accumulate as much junk as they have (they should see what I've thrown out, LOL!).

Anyhow, yesterday I found that original sheet where I wrote down what needed to be accomplished and, believe it or not, we have completed at least 85% of the things on that list. Dbaby is only 5 months old now.

It has only been a little over a month since I took Kelly up on that mission. I think God must have known that this change was coming down the road for us when He sent me to your site last November. I was able to get my routines in place before the baby came so that I wouldn't be so overwhelmed once he did arrive. And they were in place so that we were able to act on purchasing this new home (which is truly our dream home!!). Now looking back, I am sure it was God that sent me to you.

So my first thanks to God for sending you my way ... and my second thanks to you, FlyLady and Kelly, for doing God's work!!!

Jennifer from Ohio

17 Conclusion— Marla's Closing Thoughts, "From My Heart to Yours"

Here are some of my own beliefs that have sustained me:

- God is love and love is the overriding power that holds the universe together.
- If we have been beaten down for a long time, we feel unworthy of any love, especially our own.
- This lack of self-love pushes everything away from us, our family and friends, and we even push God away. Still, He always loves us.
- We too frequently act as a martyr. We may think that selfless acts bring us closer to God when, in fact, many times it is our egos that created these "selfless acts"! You shame others by saying: "Just look at what I do for you!" You carry out these acts with anger: "No one else will do this; looks like it's left up to me!" And with pride: "No one can do it as well as I can!" Oh, and let's not forget greed: "I am going to do this because I will get points and everyone will notice what I do." This attitude steals from others the ability to contribute.

219

- When we love ourselves, we do so for the joy of doing and out of love for our brethren. Everyone is blessed. How many times have you volunteered for something while your home was a disaster and you were so burnt out that you could barely function? You did not love yourself when you did these things.

- We are commanded to love our neighbor as ourselves. Did you know that if you don't love yourself first, you can't love your neighbor to the fullest extent?

- We have not been taught to love ourselves. We are told from a very early age that giving is the only way to play. There is a difference between being selfish and loving yourself. If you give away your whole pie, you are not even going to know what kind of pie you had. Save some of it for yourself so you can replenish your pie from time to time. This way you will have more to give away. Motivational speaker Rita Davenport taught me this.

- When you finally start to love yourself, your cup of love will be overflowing all the time. Love will be all around you. Love of self allows you love others more fully.

- I believe God sees us as His babies. Can you imagine God looking down on His crying babies and saying, "You are not worthy of my love"? Do you do this with your sweet babies sitting on the floor with their arms stretched up toward you? No you don't. You pick up those little darlings and cuddle them and tell them just how much you love them. Why can't you do this for yourself?

- The opposite of Love is not Hate; it is Fear. This is our perfectionism again. Fear we cannot do things right. Fear of what others will think of us. Fear that we are not good enough. When you love yourself, this fear goes away.

- Think about how much good you can do if you have more love, more time and more money. When you take care of and love yourself, all of this comes together. You will have more money because you will respect what you have and, therefore, bring more abundance into your life. You will have more time because you will be using yours wisely by taking care of yourself and your family first. Then you will have more love because the act of caring for yourself allows you to live in a loving spirit that is always filled to overflowing.

"As you spread your wings to FLY, you are opening your arms to hug the world!"

- Finally Loving Yourself is the answer to being all that you can be in God's eyes. When you can put yourself first, without guilt, you will be more able to love unconditionally. Your love will be in everything you do. You will be the reflection of the love that God has for you.

I hope you are now ready to FLY. Come join me. There is so much love to give!

I want to add a few more thoughts to my feelings above: My Sweet Darling along with Kelly and Cindy asked me how I was going to end this book. I realize every book needs a good ending and the books we love the most in our lives have touched our souls in some way. There is no ending except to say that I see this book as a beginning to a life of peace and joy.

If you put into practice what I have taught you in this book, you will be setting out on your journey, just as I have. Now you have me in puddles once again.

I never dreamed in December of 1999 that I could help one person, let alone thousands. My passion has always been to find joy in everything that I do. The joy that has filled my heart comes from you. As I have read your testimonials and have seen the changes that you have implemented in your lives, that is all I ever needed to keep me going. Your messages were the hugs and encouragement to keep me pursuing my love of helping you. Each and every one of you has touched my heart and brought tears to my eyes. You have been my guide.

My new life began January 1, 1999, when I decided for the last time to get myself organized. I had no clue that my journey would take me to you or any other place. As I gave myself and my family the gift of a comfortable home, I was able to put my sails up and let the God Breezes fill them. With my sails ready to power my ship, I followed where the Breezes took me. I am still amazed at how wonderful my home looks when I open my eyes each morning.

When I see my smile and my reflection in my shiny sink, it tells me that all is right with the world. When I look back at the last few years, I am astonished at how time FLYs when you are having fun. I guess my whole life has been in search of you and I didn't even know it. Every struggle, pain, conflict, and happiness has prepared me for my passion of helping you. I would have never been acceptable in your eyes if I had always known how to take care of my home and myself.

We know the story that when the student is ready the teacher will come. Let me turn that around a bit. When the teacher is ready to share her story, after many years of pain and sorrow, then the students will come. Also, by practicing what I preach and letting you know that I am not perfect and I will never be, I've encouraged you to identify with me.

I am one of you. I know your heart and I have felt your sadness at not living up to your unrealistic expectations. When I finally quit beating myself up for what I didn't do and started doing what I could, acceptance of myself was the spark that kept me alive. If I teach you nothing else from this book, the website, and our e-mail messages, it is that Finally Loving Yourself is your ticket to FLY! My ticket has taken me farther than my wildest dreams.

Now, with tears streaming down my face, I am here to tell you that I am just a plain ole country girl that has been FLYing by the seat of my pants and I will continue to keep my sails up and go where God's Breezes take me. All I ever wanted to do was help one person.

I love you all.

—FlyLady

"I *am* so proud of you!"

"Now that you've finished this book, don't crash and burn. Remember that you are never behind. Jump in where you are. BabySteps."

FLY Notes

*"Start writing your
routines here."*

FLY Notes

FLY Notes

FLY Notes

FLY Notes

FLY Notes